MARRIAGE BONDS
and
MINISTERS' RETURNS
of
FREDERICKSBURG, VIRGINIA
1782–1850
also
TOMBSTONE INSCRIPTIONS
from
ST. GEORGE CEMETERY
1752–1920

EDITED & PUBLISHED
by
CATHERINE LINDSAY KNORR

Please direct all Correspondence & Orders to:

Southern Historical Press, Inc.
PO Box 1267
375 W Broad Street
Southern Historical Press, Inc.
Greenville, S.C. 29602-1267

Originally Copyrighted: Catherine Lindsay Knorr, 1954
Copyright Transferred: Southern Historical Press, Inc. 1982
ISBN 978-0-89308-254-3
Printed in the United States of America

TO

THE MEMORY OF

MRS. GEORGE PHILLIPS KING

(CORA MAY HARRISON)

1882 - 1944

FOR WHOSE PLEASURE

THESE DATA WERE

ORIGINALLY GATHERED

FOREWORD

In October 1950 Mr. George Harrison Sanford King of Fredericksburg, Virginia, wrote me thanking me for two complimentary copies of my marriages of Prince Edward County, Virginia, one for himself and one for the files of the Order of First Families of Virginia of which society he was then Registrar.

In the same letter Mr. King generously offered to me his compilation of the Marriage Bonds of Fredericksburg, 1782 - 1850, to publish as one of my series of Virginia County Marriages. This volume also contained the tombstone inscriptions from Saint George's Churchyard, Fredericksburg. To his original manuscript Mr. King has added numerous bonds which were found later.

To incorporate the later findings in the body of the book I copied all marriages on 3x5 cards, alphabetized them and made a new index. The tombstone inscriptions are not indexed, but, since they are alphabetically arranged, there is no need to index them.

Since I accepted Mr. King's offer he has checked and rechecked all contents of his type written volume, particularly the later additions. Mr. King said in part:

"There never was any book of marriage records prior to 1850 and these bonds, which I have worked into a volume, are little pieces of paper, often times with the "consent" on the back or on another piece of paper, folded in. They are all the more valuable, too, because many from Caroline, Stafford, etc., where the records are destroyed, seem to have gotten the bonds for marriage here in Fredericksburg."

Later, at my request, he wrote me the following data to put in my announcement which I repeat here:

"Fredericksburg was laid out by legislative act Feb 1727(4Hening 234) from 50 acres of land then within the bounds of Spotsylvania County, on the south side of the Rappahannock River, just below the falls thereof. It was thus at the head of navigation, and from this date until the development of the railroad, was an important sea-port for ocean-going vessels of heavy burthen.

By the time of the Revolution it was a town of importance and shortly thereafter Fredericksburg was made a Corporation and completely severed from the County of Spotsylvania and authorized to have a court house of its own. The first court for the newly formed corporation was held 15 April 1782 and the marriage records date from this year (see Wm. Pennock,1782).

As Fredericksburg was the chief trading center for a large area, and in 1789 became also the seat of the Fredericksburg District Court, there was much coming and going. In this manner these marriage records actually cover a far wider area than the Corporate limits of the Town of Fredericksburg."

This is genealogical reciprocity at its highest level. Mr. King and I are both vitally interested in Virginia source material; in seeing the amount made available to the public grow and grow.

Catherine Lindsay Knorr

Catherine Lindsay Knorr

Mrs. H. A. Knorr
1401 Linden Street
Pine Bluff, Arkansas

ORIGINAL PREFACE

The Marriage Bonds here presented have been compiled from the loose papers of the Corporation Court of Fredericksburg, Virginia, and put in this form for sake of expediating the index. I wish it were possible to reproduce each bond verbatim and each little slip of paper which was found with some of the bonds on which "consent" was given by the parent or guardian. These add a peronal touch and many are quaintly phrased.

For the benefit of those who are not acquainted with the phraseology of a marriage bond the following is given as an example:

Know all Men by these Presents that we Dennis Callahan and John Atkinson are held and firmly bound unto his Excellency Edm^d. Randolph Esqr., Governor of the Commonwealth of Virginia & his successors in the sum of Fifty Pounds the Payment whereof will & truly to be made We bind ourselves our Heirs Exors: &c Jointly & severally firmly by these presents with our seals and Dated the 27th Day of December 1786.

The Condition of the above Obligation is such that Whereas there is a marriage shortly intended to be had and soleminized between the above Dennis Callahan and Margaret Atkinson If there shall be no lawful Cause to obstruct, then this obligation to be void- Else to remain in full force & Virtue -

Dennis Callaghan   *Seal*

John Atkinson   *Seal*

Usually the bondsman was a family connection of either the bridegroom or bride.

If the bride's father was the bondsman it was not necessary to obtain his written consent, for indeed his action in signing the bond as "bondsman" is evidence in itself that the marriage had his sanction.

Unless these abstracts postively state a family relationship, same is not stated on the original papers, and persons are warned against presuming, for instance, that the above John Atkinson, bondsman, was the father of Margaret Atkinson, as this genealogical relationship is not stated nor is it indicated. It simply furnishes a clue for further research.

Oftentimes the name is written by the clerk in the body of the bond using a different spelling than appears in the signature. This is to be noted in the example given above. When the spelling varies, notes have been included to call attention to this fact.

As the bride did not sign the bond her name oftentimes appears but once on the bond and this was written by the clerk. Taking into consideration the variance in spelling the names of men in the body of the bond and their signatures, it seems that the clerk did not often inquire how a name was spelled but wrote it as he saw fit at the moment. Some of the writing is very difficult to accurately decipher, and when a bride's name appears but once in the instrument it is sometimes very difficult to positively determine what was intended. When there was a question in my mind, a question mark has been inserted.

These bonds were written by the clerk. Henry Armistead, Esq., was clerk 1782-1787, in which year he died, 1787. In August, 1787, John Chew, Jr. was appointed clerk. He served until 1806 when his son Col. Robt. S. Chew assumed the office. Upon his death in 1826, his son John James Chew became clerk and served until 1867. Consequently during the period these bonds were written, except for five years, the clerk was a Mr. Chew. We therefore note Mr. Chew often appears as bondsman on the marriage bonds, and the presence of his name must not lead us to believe there was a family connection.

After the Clerk of the Court had issued a bond for the marriage of a man and woman, the minister who performed the ceremony was required by law to make periodical returns to the clerk giving the names of the contracting parties and the date the marriage was solemnized.

However we find few "returns" filed in comparison with the number of bonds issued during the period 1781-1850. It seems that the ministers were very forgetful about this matter and some of them in their notes to the clerk apologize for their procrastination.

In checking over the "returns" filed, I find several marriages which were solemnized in Fredericksburg but the bonds authorizing the said marriages have not been located. If they ever existed they are not now among the marriage bonds.

George H. S. King

Fredericksburg, Va.
January, 1942

MARRIAGES OF FREDERICKSBURG, VIRGINIA

1782 - 1850

18 May 1842. Andrew B. ADAMS and Mary Ann Currell. Sur. Granville Gilman.

17 November 1841. John ADAMS and Malvina Garnett. Sur. Hezekiah Garnett. Minister's returns say John Q Adams.

12 February 1850. Robert W. ADAMS and Ann N. Williams. Sur. William S. Chesley.

17 April 1816. Solomon ADAMS and Mary Teasley. Sur. Alexander Walker. Signature of groom the same as the one on the following bond.

16 February 1820. Solomon ADAMS and Frances Ferneyhough. Sur. John Ferneyhough who makes oath Frances is over 21.

19 August 1824. William ADAMS and Mary Ann Richardson. Sur. James Walker Lucas who makes oath Mary Ann is over 21.

19 January 1843. Thomas S. ALCOCKE and Julianna W. Johnston. Sur. Hay B. Hoomes.

3 April 1832. John B. ALEXANDER and Mary Haner. Sur. Peyton Hough.

5 October 1842. Robert H. ALEXANDER and Margaret G. Timberlake. Sur. Gabriel Johnston.

18 January 1831. Jeremiah ALLEN and Mary Stribling. Sur. Lewis Burk.

28 January 1846. Oswell S. ALLEN and Caroline Crawford. Sur. A. J. Stout.

5 July 1844. Richard ALLEN and Ellen Lewis, ward of Elizabeth Mulvey who is surety.

11 November 1829. George ALOR and Ann English, dau. Elizabeth English who makes oath Ann is over 21. Elizabeth Godfrey makes oath George is over 21. She spells the name Aylor. Sur. Henry T. Phillips.

20 October 1827. Michael AMES and Snnoy (Snowey) English, dau. of Elizabeth English who makes oath Snowey is over 21. Sur. Henry T. Phillips.

5 June 1811. Darlin ANDERSON and Sally Keeton, dau. Garrott Keeton who is surety.

12 October 1806. William ANDERSON and Elizabeth Lawson. Sur. William James.

21 April 1830. James K. APPLE and Elinor Riley. Sur. George W. Eve.

1 March 1841. Christopher Hughes ARMISTEAD and Agnes Campbell Gordon. Sur. Wellington Gordon.

11 May 1843. James ASHBY and Sarah Jane Jarvis. Sur. William N. McKenney.

19 March 1811. Vivian ASHBY and Margaret R. Skaggs. Sur. Lawrence L. Boores. Name on bond is Biven Ashby.

28 December 1847. William ATKINS and Elizabeth Layton. Sur. G. Edrington.

27 June 1843. Joseph M. ATKINSON and Sally Page Wellford. Sur. William A. Little.

3 September 1844. Peter ATWELL and Sarah Ann Richardson. Sur. Joseph Richardson who makes oath Sarah Ann is over 21.

10 September 1833. Peter ATWELL and Maria Moore. Sur. George De Baptiste.

8 July 1819. Kosciusko AUSTICE and Judith Clark, dau. of Charles Clark who is surety.

5 June 1843. Aloysius G. BAGGETT and Frances Gore. Sur. Jacob Gore.

27 November 1811. Charles BAGGETT and Eleanor Baggett. Sur. George Baggott.

12 August 1810. George BAGGOTT, JR. and Frances Whiting, dau. of Mary Whiting who consents. Sur. John Whiting. George Baggott, Jr., son of James Baggott who consents. Married 22 August.

25 December 1784. John BAGGOTT and Mary Taylor. Sur. John Benson.

5 September 1844. Samuel J. BAGGETT and Elizabeth W. Parker. Sur. Frances J. Wiatt who makes oath Elizabeth is over 21.

30 April 1833. William M. BAGGETT and Ann Elizabeth H. Gore. Sur. Jacob Gore.

26 December 1812. William BALFOUR and Polly Nicklens, dau. of Frances Nicklens who consents. Sur. John Hall. Contracting parties "Free persons of colour".

15 October 1829. Dr. William BANKHEAD and Dorothy Brayne Minor. Sur. Francis W. Taliaferro and William G. Minor.

28 February 1816. Joseph BARCLAY and Mary Lee, widow. Sur. Edward Shaw.

13 September 1828. Benjamin N. BARNETT and Judith A. Benson. Sur. Peter Hord. Signature of groom identical with the following bond.

28 September 1831. Benjamin N. BARNETT and Harriott Hord. Sur. John James Chew.

15 September 1831. Richards BARNET and Julia Miller Johnston, ward of Richard Johnston. Sur. C. E. B. Strode.

25 April 1804. Seth BARTON and Mary B. Chew. Sur. John Chew.

19 January 1820. Thomas B. BARTON and Susan C. Stone. Sur. William F. Phillips.

17 October 1832. Anthony BASCOE and Nancy Dade. Sur. John James Chew.

1 August 1826. George W. BASSETT and Betty B. Lewis. Sur. Robert Lewis.

19 November 1840. Anson BATES and Louisa C. T. Garnett. Sur. John Ferneyhough who makes oath Louisa is over 21.

2 February 1805. James BATES and Mary Lymbrick. Sur. Porch Lymbrick. He signs, oddly, James Baets.

17 November 1840. William H. BATES and Nancy Hewlett. Sur. Peter Hazelgrove. John L. Sibley makes oath that both parties are over 21.

2 November 1836. Richard T. BAXTER and Fanny Kenny. Sur. William B. Hore.

30 May 1836. Thornton BAXTER and Maria Sparks. Sur. Thornton Taylor who makes oath Maria is over 21.

13 July 1815. William BAYNHAM and Polly De Baptist, dau. of John De Baptist, deceased, and Frances De Baptist. Sur. Benjamin De Baptist.

19 February 1834. William C. BEALE and Jane B. Howison. Sur. Samuel Howison.

5 March 1847. Morris B. BECK and Sarah A. Hanson. Sur. Sidney H. Owens.

23 May 1837. James A. BECKHAM and Frances J. Alcocke, dau. of E. S. Alcocke who consents. Sur. John James Chew.

11 October 1843. John BECKLEY and Clara Webb. Sur. James Mondowney.

12 July 1830. Andrew B. BECKWITH and Adelade B. Carter. Sur. James R. Johnson.

26 January 1826. Barnes BECKWITH and Elizabeth Cox. Sur. Francis Cox who makes oath Elizabeth Cox has neither parent living.

23 May 1837. Daniel BEDINGER and Catherine H. Berry. Sur. Law. (Lawrence) W. Berry.

14 May 1832. Francis H. BELL and Sarah B. Wood, dau. of Tomzin Wood. Sur. James H. Seldon.

7 October 1844. N. P. BEMIS and J. H. Stevenson. Sur. William W. Tyler.

24 October 1838. Jere BENDEN and Mary Meredith. Sur. Henry Jones.

27 December 1784. Charles BENNETT and Ann Dunn. Sur. John Davis.

3 February 1813. John B. BENSON and Christiana Yates Day, dau. of Benjamin Day who consents. Sur. Robert S. Chew.

15 August 1814. William BERNARD and Sarah Dykes. Sur. Patrick C. Robb. William Bernard son of William Bernard, Esq., of "Mannsfield" in Spottsylvania County, who writes his consent to the marriage.

3 February 1835. John J. BERRY and Mary W. Lucas. Sur. Albert G. Lucas who makes oath Mary is 21.

17 November 1825. Lawrence W. BERRY and Ann Scott. Sur. John Scott.

29 December 1829. Thomas J. BERRY and Mary Hill. Sur. Thomas G. Tupman who makes oath Mary is over 21.

4 January 1783. John BINGEY and Ruth McKnight. Sur. William Smith.

5 April 1817. Thomas BLACKBURN and Mary Ann H. Wright. Sur. Thomas Wright who makes oath Mary Ann is over 21.

8 October 1825. William M. BLACKFORD and Mary B. Minor. Sur. John Minor. Married 12 October in Hanover County, Va., by the Rev. John Cooke.

10 July 1848. Robert N. BLAKE and Mary Ann Anderson, dau. of M. D. Anderson. Sur. Lewis O. Magrath.

20 July 1843. Mitchell A. BLANKMAN and Jane B. Crawford. Sur. Edward McDowell.

12 December 1836. Robert BLOXTON and Louisa Brown, dau. of Mary L. Brown. Sur. William Fulcher, Jr.

28 June 1837. Zachariah BLOXTON and Arabella Odor. Sur. Jefferson Cowne.

25 September 1850. Stephen BOARDMAN, Jr. and Tacy A. Smith. Sur. George H. C. Rowe.

24 October 1822. Thomas H. BOTTS and Ann C. Willis. Married by the Rev. Edward C. McGuire, Rector of St. George's Parish. Ministers' returns.

10 October 1828. Thomas H. BOTTS and Mary S. Stone. Sur. William Browne.

10 December 1846. P. Alexander BOWER and Elizabeth W. Rothrock, dau. of W. C. I. Rothrock. Sur. James N. Barnett.

23 June 1825. William BOWEN and Elizabeth Young. Sur. James Young.

23 December 1847. Elijah BOWLING and Letitia Davis, dau. of Lucinda Ellis who consents. Sur. George L. Bowling.

11 May 1850. Henry BOWLING and Sarah Harris. Sur. George F. Chew.

2 December 1845. Graves BOWLING and Maria Cooper. Sur. Daniel W. Kennedy.

2 March 1837. Henry D. BOWMAN and Julia M. Magrath. Sur. Jesse Pullen.

29 December 1837. Daniel BRADFORD and Mary E. Morris. Sur. Alexander Morris.

7 March 1832. Uriah H. BRADSHAW and Jane Wright. Sur. Alexander Sorrell. Signature of groom identical with the following bond.

11 September 1843. Uriah H. BRADSHAW and Ellen B. Murray. Sur. William Murray.

18 July 1825. Joseph BRAGDON and Elizabeth Connor. Sur. Mary Connor.

27 May 1828. Richard F. BRAXTON and Nancy Calvert. Sur. Thomas Calvert.

19 December 1843. Winter BRAY and Mary Frances Dickey. Sur. Robert Dickey.

24 August 1843. Richard M. BREMMER and Angelina Portch, dau. of Prestrious Portch. Sur. Achilles A. Wrenn.

5 May 1818. George BRENT and Harriet Slater. Sur. William Wells.

9 September 1819. Thomas BRIEANA and Patsy Harpe, ward of Thomas Brieana her intended spouse. Sur. Josiah Armstrong.

19 August 1785. Charles BRIMMER and _____ Mayfield. Sur. John Mayfield.

15 January 1832. Isaiah E. BRISSEY and Agnes P. Bibb. Sur. Thomas Bibb.

13 February 1804. Francis J. BROOKE and Mary Champe Carter. Sur. Robert S. Chew.

5 January 1785. Richard BROOKE and Maria Mercer. Sur. Henry Armistead.

26 September 1844. Asaph BROWN and Henrietta H. Kendall, widow. Sur. John J. Rollow. For proof that Henrietta H. Kendall was a widow when she married Asaph Brown see the marriage of James T. Kendall 1848. Henrietta H. Browne, mother of James T. Kendall, consents.

14 October 1835. Bartlett BROWN and Peggy Mahoney. Sur. James Mills who makes oath Peggy is over 21.

17 September 1818. Carter BROWN and Judy Evans, dau. Peggy Evans. Sur. Thomas Anslow and Peggy Evans. Contracting parties "Free persons of colour".

28 February 1849. Charles G. BROWN and Ellen Douglas Ficklen. Sur. James F. Brown.

16 November 1842. Charles M. BROWN and Sophia Calhoun. Sur. L. J. Huffman.

5 August 1786. Christopher BROWN and Judith Green. Sur. John Bingey.

19 December 1850. Coleman R. BROWN and Emily M. Brown. Sur. James Waite.

7 September 1844. Nahum F. D. BROWNE and Julia McWilliams. Sur. Robert L. McGuire.

17 July 1837. Richard Lewis BROWN and Ann E. Middleton. Sur. Henry O. Middleton.

17 December 1810. William BROWN, (Free Negro) and Sally Gibbs, negro slave of Charles L. Carter who is surety.

14 December 1814. Dr. William BROWN and Margaret Emmilly Stone, dau. of W. S. Stone who writes his consent. Sur. Charles H. Smith.

23 December 1823. Robert C. BRUCE and Mary L. Young, dau. of James Young who consents. Sur. George Garnett.

26 May 1832. George BRYANT and Elizabeth Faulkner. Sur. William H. Bryant.

16 July 1803. Andrew BUCHANAN and Anne Baxter. Sur. Stephen Winchester.

24 August 1812. John H. BUCKMAN and Susanah Day, dau. of Sarah Day who consents. Sur. Michael Reader.

22 January 1847. William S. BULLOCK and Harriet Stewart. Sur. Robert B. Semple. Bernard Cole makes oath both are over 21.

1 July 1841. Muscoe BUNDY (Alias Muscoe Johnson) and Ann Maria Jackson. Sur. Robert Prim. George Williams makes oath Ann Maria is over 21.

30 December 1824. Lewis BURKE and Mary Burnley. Sur. Solomon Adams.

24 February 1848. Lewis BURKE and Eliza Terrier. Sur. Roy Jones.

2 September 1847. Thomas O. BURRUS and Lucy F. Waller, ward of Gabriel Long who consents in writing. Sur. R. B. Semple. This name is also spelled Burrows and Burroughs in this same bond.

26 September 1808. Lewis BURWELL and Maria M. Page. Sur. John T. Page.

5 December 1823. Philip BURWELL and Susan R. Wellford. Sur. John S. Wellford.

9 June 1825. John V. M. BUSKIRK and Judith Curry. Sur. John Curry who makes oath Judith is over 21.

29 June 1824. Williams BUTLER and Maria Vessells. Sur. Benjamin Parke who makes oath Maria is over 21.

10 August 1850. Thornton BYRAM and Mary E. A. Lewis. Sur. Henry Bowling.

25 November 1819. James H. CALDWELL and Maria C. Wormeley. Sur. Horace Marshall.

19 March 1834. John S. CALDWELL and Emily L. Phillips. Sur. Samuel Phillips.

7 December 1833. Richard CALDWELL and Caroline H. Verone. Sur. Robert Gray who makes oath Caroline is over 21.

27 December 1831. John CALHOUN, Jr. and Julia Ann Southard. Sur. Edmund Southard who makes oath Julia Ann is over 21.

27 December 1786. Dennis CALLAGHAN and Margaret Atkinson. Sur. John Atkinson.

31 March 1838. George CAMMACK and Barsheby Cox. Sur. William Cox who makes oath Barsheby is over 21.

30 November 1811. Donald CAMPBELL and Eliza M. Fisher. Sur. Robert Mackay.

4 June 1833. James M. CAMPBELL and Emma N. Gray. Sur. Peter Spillman.

26 December 1817. Robert CAMPBELL and Jane Ferguson. Sur. James Ferguson. Contracting parties "Free Persons of Colour".

11 September 1838. William M. CANNON and Anne E. Taylor. Sur. Libern P. Raines who makes oath Anne is over 21.

18 December 1832. Delphy CARLIN and Mary J. Chewning, dau. of John Chewning who makes oath Mary is over 21. Sur. William F. Gray. Married by the Rev. Edward C. McGuire, Rector of St. George's Parish. Delphy Carlin of Louisiana.

19 January 1830. Dr. George F. CARMICHAEL and Mary Carter Wellford, dau. of John S. Wellford who consents. Sur. E. H. Carmichael.

29 November 1850. James CARPENTER and Rebecca D. Dodd. Sur. Archibald Edmonson and William Berkely, Jr., who make oath they heard the father of Rebecca (name not stated) say she was over 21, and that he had no objection to the marriage.

19 October 1830. Edwin CARTER and Elizabeth E. P. James. Sur. Ferdinand Strother.

25 March 1812. John CARTER and Elizabeth Sterling, widow of Joseph Sterling. Sur. Frederick Pilcher.

16 April 1812. Capt. Nicholas CARTER and Patsey Taylor. Sur. John Snow. Filed with bond: "Fred g April 16, 1812, Mr. Chew, Sir: I hereby request you to grant license to join in the solemn State of Matrimony Patsy Taylor with Capt. Nicholas Carter. Wit. John Snow. Thomas Taylor".

1 May 1827. John F. CARUTHERS and Mary B. Wilson. Sur. Samuel B. Wilson.

23 May 1820. Samuel CARY and Willy M. Carter, dau. of John Carter who is surety.

17 March 1804. Thomas CARY and Sarah Rawlins. Sur. James Ferguson.

24 November 1841. Thomas CARY and Julia Richards. Sur. Henry Young.

19 August 1845. William J. CASON and Mary Eleanor Baggett. Sur. Samuel J. Bagett.

28 February 1835. George W. CHESLEY and Frances A. Kent. Sur. Robert G. Layton.

6 February 1837. Robert CHESLEY and Eliza Mills, dau. of James Mills who makes oath Robert Chesley is over 21. Married by the Rev. James D. McCabe.

14 January 1840. William S. CHESLEY and Mary Ann Ferneyhough. Sur. John Ferneyhough.

21 January 1846. James CHEVERELL and Louise Garner. Sur. John L. Sibley who makes oath both are over 21.

23 March 1825. John James CHEW and Ellen Ann Patton. Sur. Robert Patton.

21 October 1819. John W. CHEW and Ann Thornton Vass, dau. Mary Christy who consents. Sur. John T. Ford.

19 December 1843. Dr. Francis B. CHEWNING and Elizabeth H. Smith, dau. of William K. Smith who is surety.

28 December 1809. Samuel CHEWNING and Susannah Walker. Sur. Burkett Bowen.

22 December 1831. Rawleigh T. CHINN and Mary Hord (or Hore). Sur. George Rowe who makes oath Mary is over 21.

2 August 1817. Joseph CHRISTY and Mary Vass, widow. Sur. Benjamin Parke.

29 January 1845. Herbert A. CLAIBORNE, Jr. and Mary Anna McGuire. Sur. Robert L. McGuire.

2 March 1812. Robert CLARK and Mary Ann Brown. Sur. John Hunley and George Fry. John Hundley makes oath Mary Ann is over 21.

9 July 1824. Benjamin CLARKE and Elizabeth McPherson. Sur. John Robinson.

8 January 1825. Lewis CLARKE and Sarah Mitchum, widow. Sur. John S. Caldwell.

30 October 1812. Henry CLAYTON and Elizabeth Coyle, widow. Sur. Henry Raymond.

10 November 1831. John CLEMENTS and Fanny Mann. Sur. John James Chew.

23 November 1836. John COAKLEY and Elizabeth Thom. Sur. Richard H. Phillips.

11 April 1812. John A. COBB and Sarah Rootes. Sur. Thomas R. Rootes.

24 December 1827. James COGGSDALL and Mary Ann Jones, dau. of Jane Jones who writes consent. Sur. Joshua Myers.

1 November 1837. Counceller COLE and Sarah E. Carpenter, ward of Uriah H. Bradshaw who consents.

29 January 1838. Henry H. COLE and Jane Finnall, dau. of James Finnall who is surety. John Underwood makes oath Henry H. Cole is over 21.

20 December 1821, Richard L. COLEMAN and Mary Cunningham. Sur. James Cunningham, Jr., who makes oath Mary is over 21. The indenture of Richard L. Coleman is filed with his marriage bond. He was indented 12 March 1816 to John Robinson of Fredericksburg by his mother Nancy Coleman. She states in the indenture Richard will be 21 on 29 June 1821, at which time he is to be free. Robinson was to teach him the trade of a carpenter and house joiner.

29 November 1837. Albert G. COLLINS and Emily P. Bosel, dau. of Richard Bozel who writes consent. Sur. Richard Wallace.

23 June 1847. John W. COLLINS and Mary S. McKildoe. Sur. Samuel Lyell.

11 December 1816. John COMBS, alias John Fry, and Alice Ware, former servant to the late John Lear and dau. of Elzey Ware, deceased. Sur. R. S. Chew. Contracting parties "Free Persons of Colour".

12 May 1841. Edwin H. CONWAY and Fanny Scott Gregory. Sur. Charles S. Scott.

13 July 1848. William Z. COOK and Catherine Acers. Sur. Gabriel Minor who makes oath Catherine Acers is over 21 and a "Free woman of colour".

13 July 1826. James COOKE and Emily M. Pearson. Sur. Fayette Johnston. A note in the section of tombstone inscriptions says she was the daughter of William Pearson.

28 May 1803. John COPENHAGEN and Sarah Dobbs who gives own consent. Sur. James Doggett.

4 September 1849. John H. CONNER and Elizabeth Byram, dau. of Emanuel Byram who is surety.

20 April 1829. James CORBIN and Mary Jane Briscoe. Sur. William Briscoe.

19 January 1830. James P. CORBIN and Jane Catharine Wellford, dau. of John S. Wellford who writes consent. Sur. Edward H. Carmichael. James P. Corbin is ward of S. A. Storrow who writes consent.

20 October 1836. William H. COURTNEY and Susan Staylor, dau. of John Staylor who writes consent. Sur. George Ayler.

27 December 1821. Bowling COWNE and Elizabeth Copenhagen, ward of said Bowling Cowne. Sur. Joseph D. Thompson.

23 September 1815. Robert COWPER and Sophia Gaines. Sur. John A. French.

27 April 1836. Abraham COX and Ariana Caldwell. Sur. John S. Caldwell.

18 January 1830. George COX and Elizabeth Wright. Sur. William H. Wright who makes oath Elizabeth is 21.

19 December 1850. George L. COX and Elizabeth B. Beckwith, dau. of Barnes Beckwith who writes consent. Sur. George H. Peyton.

2 July 1824. John F. COX and Ann Kennedy, dau. of Hennery and Mary Kennedy who consent. Sur. Peter Cox.

29 December 1827. John G. COX and Drusilla Ames. Sur. Michael Ames who makes oath both parties are over 21. Married by the Rev. Philip D. Lipscomb.

25 December 1822. Peter P. COX and Margaret P. Bryant. Sur. Hezekiah Redder who makes oath Margaret is 21.

12 October 1831. Peter COX and Jane Finnall, dau. of Robert Finnall of Stafford Co. who consents. Sur. John J. Rollow.

1 December 1841. Robert A. COX and Maria M. Lane. Sur. Robert F. Hening who makes oath Maria is 21.

8 January 1827. William COX and Mary Ann McD. Finnall, dau. of Robert Finnall of Stafford Co. who consents. Sur. William Rollow.

1 January 1829. William COX and Maria B. King. Sur. Isaac M. King.

1 April 1807. Richard COYLE and Sally Day, dau. of Sarah Day who consents. Sur. Charles Brown.

5 December 1811. Richard COYLE and Elizabeth Hazlegrove, widow of Benjamin Hazlegrove. Sur. Peter Lucas.

28 February 1828. Dewitt C. CRAWFORD and Sarah Embrey who writes her own consent. Sur. Archibald Burden or Burton. George Crawford makes oath his son Dewitt C. Crawford is 24 years old next May.

19 May 1847. John CREIGHTON and Jane Barrett. Sur. George H. Peyton.

1 August 1849. Jacob H. CRIDLIN and Harriet Southard. Sur. James Southard who makes oath Harriet is 21.

2 April 1807. Thomas CROSLEY and Dorothea J. Taylor, dau. of Thomas Taylor who consents. Sur. Thomas Kent. Ministers' returns say Crossly.

30 April 1818. Capt. William CROSSBY and Mary Garton. Sur. Lindsey Pullen. See William Crossley.

30 April 1818. William CROSSLEY and Mary Garton. Married by the Rev. Edward C. McGuire, Rector of St. George's Parish. See William Crossby.

16 February 1826. Timothy CROWLEY and Ann Bloxton. Jesse Curtis makes oath Ann is 21.

8 February 1809. Reubin CRUMP and Mary Green. Sur. William Alexander.

24 May 1832. Robert H. CRUMP and Selina M. Ellis. Sur. Robert W. Hart.

11 July 1836. William CRUMP, Jr. and Ann Eliza Dickey. Sur. Robert Dickey.

1 December 1820. Thomas CUMMINGS and Sarah Harvey. Sur. William Warren who makes oath Sarah is "considerably over 21".

13 December 1819. George CUNNINGHAM and Malvina P. Staiar, dau. of Jacob Staiar who is surety.

29 December 1819. James CUNNINGHAM and Mary Ann Helmstetter. Sur. James Harrison who makes oath Mary Ann is 21.

26 April 1837. John CUPPENHAVER and Mary Calhoun, dau. Mary Calhoun who writes consent. Sur. George B. Waite.

28 July 1828. Henry CURRELL and Nancy Barrett. Sur. Henry T. Phillips and Benjamin Parke.

15 December 1836. John B. CURRELL and Mary Ann Myers, dau. of Mrs. Sarah Myers who makes oath Mary Ann was 21 "June last". Sur. Charles C. Wellford.

2 October 1819. James CURRIE and Elizabeth Jett, dau. of George Jett who is surety. Married by the Rev. William James.

8 April 1841. Stephen C. CURRY and Maria E. Mullen, dau. of Ellen Mullen who writes consent. Sur. Ryland Mullen.

28 October 1842. Elijah CURTIS and Polly Couwne?. Sur. Abraham Howard.

6 July 1826. Jesse CURTIS and Elizabeth Milna. Sur. John S. Caldwell.

6 May 1820. Stiles P. CURTIS and Ann Brown Jones, dau. of Mrs. Philadelphia Jones who makes oath her daughter is 21. Sur. John Robinson.

19 June 1822. Thomas CURTIS and Ann Gray, ward of said Thomas Curtis. Sur. Peter P. Cox.

12 February 1816. John DABNEY and Sarah King. Henry and Ellener King write consent, no relationship stated. Sur. John Hunley.

24 June 1818. William DABNEY and Lucy Layton, dau. of John Layton, Sr. who consents. Sur. Thomas Jennings.

14 March 1838. Edward DAINGERFIELD and Adelaide Payne, dau. of Catherine Fulcher, formerly Payne who consents. Sur. William Edwards.

5 November 1804. John DAINGERFIELD and Eleanor B. Armistead, ward of David C. Kerr who is surety.

13 February 1830. John T. DANIEL and Harriet W. Fitzhugh, ward of Frances T. Fitzhugh. Sur. John James Chew.

27 May 1835. Thomas R. DANIEL and Frances Smith. Sur. Jacob Grotz who makes oath. Frances is 21.

1 May 1833. Rev. John LeRoy DAVIES and Eliza Chew Gordon Wilson, dau. of Rev. Samuel B. Wilson who consents and is surety.

9 April 1834. Addison L. DAVIS and Dorothea Ann Farish, dau. of Johnston Farish who consents. Sur. Robert Wright.

8 August 1839. Gustavus R. DAVIS and Mary M. Kelly. Sur. William H. Murphy.

23 January 1845. William E. DAVIS and Elizabeth Miffline. Sur. Charles C. Wellford.

15 October 1832. Frederick DAWSON and Patsey White. Sur. Stephen Young.

18 November 1818. Edward De BAPTIST and Henrietta Jordone, dau. of Betsy Jordine who makes oath Henrietta is 21. Sur. Alexander Duncan.

18 June 1831. William De BAPTIST and Eliza Lewis. Sur. William Duncan.

11 December 1823. Robert DEDMAN and Elizabeth J. Timberlake. Sur. Thomas B. Adams.

28 October 1844. Daniel S. DELAPLANE and Mary A. Pilcher. Sur. Sidney H. Owen.

29 April 1850. William H. DERR and Frances Thomas. Sur. Arthur Jenkins who makes oath Frances is 21.

18 February 1825. Daniel DEMPSEY and Mary Fountain. Sur. Horace Clark. She writes her own consent saying she is "of lawful age having a daughter nearly marriageable," signed Polly Fountain. Wit. Thomas S. Clark and Daniel Davis.

30 September 1814. Amos S. DENORMANDIE and Elizabeth H. Stone, dau. of William G. Stone who is surety.

19 June 1817. Robert DICKEY and Eliza Slater. Sur. Thomas Proctor.

17 May 1837. Robert DICKEY and Elizabeth Paull. Sur. A. K. Phillips. Married by the Rev. James D. McCabe.

26 October 1844. James E. DICKINSON and Ellen C. Middleton. Sur. William T. Hart.

27 June 1810. John W. DITMAN and Grace Calhoun, widow. Sur. David C. Coyle.

2 August 1812. Thomas DODSON and Catherine Webster. Sur. William Wines who makes oath Catherine is 21. Bond reads "Soldier".

26 December 1827. Samuel DOGGETT and Maria Wilson. Sur. Boling Coon, who makes oath both are 21.

15 November 1828. Wishart DOGGETT and Harriett Courtney. Sur. Samuel Thompson. Wishart Doggett ward of Horace Marshall who consents.

7 August 1837. James DONAHOE and Mary Faulkner. Sur. John A. Taylor who makes oath both are 21.

23 July 1832. Joshua DONAHOE and Lavinia Powell. Sur. Richard Caldwell.

8 February 1848. Joshua DONAHOE and Margarett W. Adams. Sur. George B. Waite.

6 November 1783. Christopher DONALY and Suckey Moor. Sur. John McKenney. She writes her own consent.

13 October 1817. Isaac DONELLE and Sarah Shears. Sur. William Wells. Isaac Donelle son of Andrew Donelle who consents. Susan Buckman makes oath Sarah is 21.

1 November 1819. George DONIPHAN and Harriet Victor. Sur. Benjamin Clark.

3 April 1827. Henry R. DULANEY and Fanny A. Carter. Sur. John Minor.

12 March 1813. Alexander DUNCAN, Jr. and Fanny More, "a mulatto girl
formerly the property of Edward More, deceased, of Stafford County
who was legally emancipated in April 1806 as appears recorded in Stafford Court". Signed by Samuel Howison. Alexander Duncan, Sr. consents
to his son's marriage. "Free persons of colour".

18 June 1836. Richard EATON and Catherine Hughlett. Sur. Richard J.
Tutt. Catherine writs her own consent stating she has been "left
without parents and is of lawful age." Signed Catherine C. Hughlett.
Wit. " My friend, Pressella Donalson, June 17th, 1836.

30 September 1830. H. J. EDES and Ann Kelley. Sur. William Warren.

15 June 1836. Gilford EDINGTON and Lucinda Perry. Sur. Stewart
Roughton.

25 October 1843. Vincent N. EDMONDS and Sarah Franklin Haywood, dau.
of Julia Ann Haywood who consents. Sur. Samuel D. Curtis.

19 April 1842. Archibald EDMONDSON and Eliza Ann Williams. Sur. John
King.

11 March 1847. John M. EDRINGTON and Sophia A. Withers. Sur. William
H. Stephens.

21 April 1818. Enoch EDWARDS and Ann Newton, widow, writes her own
consent. Sur. Thomas Edwards.

1 March 1837. William EDWARDS and Ann Payne. Sur. William Fulcher,Jr.
Dau. of Catherine Fulcher formerly Catherine Payne, who writes consent.
Wit. William Fulcher, Jr., and Daniel Norris.

13 December 1842. Perry I. (or J.) EGGBORNE and Martha P. Redd, dau.
of W. Redd who consents. Sur. Hugh Scott.

2 June 1817. Capt. Edward EGGLESTON and Matilda H. Maury. Capt.
Eggleston of Amelia County. Married by the Rev. Edward C. McGuire,
Rector of St. George's Parish. Ministers' returns.

27 June 1825. William Alexander ELIASON and Mary L. Carter. Sur.
John Minor who makes oath Mary is 21.

10 August 1837. J. M. W. ELLIOTT and Frances E. Smith. Sur. A. W.
Wrenn.

7 March 1829. John W. ELLIS and Harriet H. Wardell. Sur. George
Mitchell.

10 July 1815. Edward ELLY and Sarah Jones, dau. of Isaac Jones who is
surety.

27 March 1816. Thomas M. EMERSON and Alice Lear. See Thomas M. Everson. Virginia Herald March 30th 1816.

20 May 1841. John A. ENGLISH and Judith B. Jones, ward of Stiles P. Curtis who consents. Sur. Argalus E. Samuel.

5 November 1803. William ENGLISH and Eliza Collawn, widow. Sur. Walter Gregory.

24 December 1803. Benjamin ESSEX and Ann Simpson, relict, who writes her own consent. Sur. William Smith.

9 June 1818. Triplett T. ESTES and Hannah Lee Basye. Sur. George Baggott.

26 August 1840. John EUBANK and Elizabeth Long. Sur. Charles Bayley.

21 November 1837. William C. EUSTACE and Mary L. Tomlin. Ann C. Tomlin, mother of Mary L. Tomlin gives her consent to the marriage, stating said Mary L. "is the infant orphan of the late Williamson B. Tomlin". Sur. William Storke. William C. Eustace of Lancaster County.

9 November 1819. John EVANS and Betsy Tombs, dau. of Marietta Lewis who is surety. Contracting parties "Free persons of colour".

15 June 1841. Robert EVANS and Ellen Lucas. Sur. James West, Jr.

25 November 1828. George W. EVE and Elizabeth Sanger. Sur. Richard Caldwell.

27 March 1816. Thomas M. EVERSON and Alice Lear. Sur. Benjamin Clark. See Thomas M. Emerson.

15 June 1807. Amos FAULKNER and Nancy Sullivan who writes her consent to license being issued saying she is 26 years of age. Sur. Daniel Mathews.

9 May 1821. William FAULKNER and Mary Lewis, dau. of Willis Lewis. Sur. Jesse Wayt.

14 November 1809. James FERGUSON and Polly Mann. Sur. Armistead Stocus.

21 November 1843. Joseph FERGUSON and Evelina Richards. Sur. Adolph Richards.

3 April 1830. Gustavus FERRELL and Nancy Chandler. Sur. Benjamin R. Hillyard. This name also appears as Feraile on this marriage bond.

1 November 1847. John F. FICKLIN and Sarah A. Slaughter. Sur. F. Slaughter.

1 February 1830. Thomas FINNAL and Ann F. Bullard, dau. of Judith Bullard who writes her consent. Sur. William Cox. Thomas Finnal son of Robert Finnal who writes his consent to the marriage.

28 February 1839. Daniel FITCHETT and Cordelia Jenkins. Tascoe Jenkins makes oath Cordelia is over 21. Sur. John B. Currell.

8 February 1849. James E. FITCHETT and Lucinda Perry. Sur. George H. Peyton.

9 January 1810. John FITCHETT and Ann Cayloe, dau. of Mary Ann Cayloe who writes her consent. Sur. John Murphy.

19 January 1830. John FITCHETT and Sally Downting who writes her own consent. Sur. George Reveer.

20 September 1847. John FITCHETT and Martha Ann Stone. Sur. E. E. True.

2 December 1835. William FITCHETT and Clarissa Holbrook. Sur. Stewart Roughton.

15 September 1824. McCarty FITZHUGH and Lucinda De Baptist. Sur. Henry Moore.

18 July 1820. William D. FITZHUGH and Martha S. Thornton. Married by the Rev. Edward C. McGuire, Rector of St. George's Parish. Ministers' returns.

23 February 1847. William FITZHUGH and Elizabeth Lucas. Sur. Henry Lucas.

14 February 1812. Baldwin FLETCHER and Elizabeth Williams. Sur. William Williams.

17 February 1810. John Taylor FORD and Patsey Gregory, dau. of Walter Gregory who consents and is surety.

25 August 1835. Owen J. FOULKE and Elizabeth Pusey. Sur. William Mills.

24 October 1836. Thornton FOX and Ann West. Sur. Adolph Richards.

16 November 1829. William FRANKLIN and Mary Terrier. Sur. Daniel G. Read.

22 March 1810. James FRENCH and Elizabeth Chew. Married by the Rev. S. B. Wilson. Ministers' returns

17 July 1841. Michael FRENCH and Philippa C. Burton, dau. of Charles Burton who consents. Sur. H. A. Williams.

23 January 1812. William FRENCH and Elizabeth Barton, dau. of Seth Barton who is surety.

10 March 1825. Enoch FRITTER and Polly Knight. Sur. Lemuel Thompson.

26 December 1820. Hugh W. FRY and Maria White, dau. of Henry White who is surety.

27 November 1845. James S. FUGETT and Elizabeth T. Clift. Sur. Thomas Sullivan.

11 November 1847. James S. FUGITT and Rebecca M. Henry. Sur. Ro. B. Semple. Signature on bond is identical with the one above except for the e in one and the i in the other. Probably the same man.

13 September 1828. William FULCHER, Jr., and Catherine Payne who writes her own consent saying she is over 21. Sur. Peter Rollow.

2 April 1850. Francis GAINES and Maria Sales. Sur. James Morton.

1 December 1842. Andrew GARRION and Ann T. Phillips. Sur. John Crosley.

27 February 1840. Hezekiah GARNER and Eliza Mullen. Sur. Henry Mullin who makes oath both parties are over 21.

8 February 1843. Mason GARNER and Louise Donalson, dau. of Priscilla Donalson who consents. Sur. Peter Hazelgrove. Mason Garner son of Travers Garner of Stafford Co. who writes his consent.

9 January 1845. Robert GARNER and Unus Layton. Sur. Travers Garner who makes oath both are over 21.

20 May 1811. George GARNETT and Fanny B. Banks, dau. of Gerard Banks who is surety.

16 July 1845. Reuben M. GARNETT and Elizabeth Allen Williams, dau. of James Williams. Sur. James A. Williams. Reuben M. Garnett of King and Queen Co.

30 April 1833. John B. GARRETT and Elizabeth Ann Walker. Sur. William Bowen.

11 July 1817. Hancock GASKINS and Mary Rasor. Sur. Thomas Proctor.

15 August 1833. James GATTIN and Eliza Bundy. Sur. Fanny Levie.

14 October 1835. Henry D. GENTHER and Eliza Ann Rollow. Sur. John L. Shultice.

27 July 1836. Moses GEORGE and Betsy Fichett. Sur. John Fichett.

28 July 1783. William GEORGE and Flora McKeen. Sur. William Holderby.

1 October 1812. Charley GEYER and Elizabeth Jackson, widow. Sur. Charles Clark.

20 July 1842. John GILHAM and Mary Riley. Sur. John S. G. Timberlake who makes oath both parties are over 21.

11 November 1841. Charles R. GILL and Adeline Towles. Sur. Henry D. Genther.

23 April 1838. James Lindsey GILLESPIE and Mary Harrison Hall. Sur. John B. Hall.

30 December 1830. Granville GILLMAN and Mary Ann Jones, dau. of Jane Jones who consents. Sur. George Alor.

12 September 1827. John GLASCOCK and Agnes Davis. Sur. Daniel Davis.

11 October 1837. Michael C. GLASSETT and Mary Ann Burke. Sur. Lewis Burke.

20 February 1817. Augustine GODEFREY and Elizabeth Williams, widow. Sur. George Fry. He apparently signs in German.

4 September 1817. David GOLDSBY and Mitilda Howard, dau. of William Howard who is surety.

21 August 1850. William GOODRICK and Mary Currell. Sur. James Raines.

16 October 1834. Arthur GOODWIN and Ann Thom. Sur. John Catesby Thom.

21 December 1819. Charles GOODWIN and Jannett Gordon Carmichael, dau. of James Carmichael who consents. Sur. Archibald Hart.

19 December 1838. John Thomas GOODWIN and Ann Elizabeth Goodwin, dau. of W. P. Goodwin who consents. Sur. John H. Goodwin. John Thomas Goodwin ward of Elizabeth D. Goodwin who consents.

30 October 1832. Littleton GOODWIN and Ann Maria Smock. Married by the Rev. Edward C. McGuire, Rector of St. George's Parish. Ministers' returns.

26 September 1816. William P. GOODWIN and Caroline Heiskell. Sur. H. Marhsall.

24 April 1827. William P. GOODWIN and Mary B. Burke, widow of William Burke, nee Crutchfield. Sur. Arthur Goodwin. See Tod vs. Goodwin. File 309 F.D.C.

5 November 1824. Alexander GORDON and Susan F. Gordon, dau. of Samuel Gordon who writes his consent from "Kenmore" near Fredericksburg, Sur. William A. Knox.

16 October 1845. James L. GORDON and Mary F. Beale. Sur. William C. Beale.

5 November 1846. Reuben L. GORDON and Eliza S. Beale. Sur. William C. Beale.

17 February 1808. William GORDON and Rebecca Cooke, dau. of John Cooke who consents. Sur. Adam Cooke. Married by the Rev. S. B. Wilson.

14 December 1809. William F. GORDON and Mary R. Rootes. Sur. William A. Gregory.

11 December 1833. Charles W. GORE and Elizabeth Pullin, sister of Jesse Pullin who is surety and makes oath Elizabeth is over 21.

1 November 1808. Jacob GORE and Elizabeth Hildrup. Sur. Joseph Walker who makes oath Elizabeth is over 21.

30 March 1833. John H. GORE and Jane F. Wood. Sur. Francis H. Bell. Tomzin Wood consents but no relationship is stated.

13 June 1844. Caleb GORSUCH and Mary Virginia Gibbs, dau. of Mary A. Gibbs who consents. Sur. George B. Waite.

20 Mary 1845. James S. GRAHAM and Angelina S. Finnall. Sur. Walter H. Finnall.

16 October 1821. Aitcheson GRAY and Catharine D. Willis. Sur. Byrd C. Willis.

24 October 1829. John Bowie GRAY and Jane Cave, ward of Jeremiah Morton who consents. Sur. William Pollock. John Bowie Gray of "Traveller's Rest" Stafford Co.

19 November 1829. Thomas W. GRAY and Sally Lucas. Sur. Fielding Lucas.

24 September 1817. William F. GRAY and Milly Richards Stone, dau. of M. S. Stone who consents. Sur. John W. Green.

14 April 1836. George GRAVATT and Mary S. Long, dau. of Joshua Long who consents. Sur. John Rollow.

24 December 1805. John W. GREEN and Mary Brown. Sur. Robert Hening.

26 October 1821. Jones GREEN and Susanna E. M. Scott. Sur. Thomas Hord.

29 September 1841. Leavell GREEN and Delia Fitchett. Sur. Gilford Eddington.

7 June 1817. Timothy GREEN and Lucy Carter. Sur. John T. Ford.

4 February 1817. Charles GREGORY and Sophia P. Hall. Sur. Byrd C. Willis.

12 September 1819. Walter GREGORY and Alzira Smith, widow. Sur. Robert Parrott.

18 December 1818. William A. GREGORY and Willa S. Maury. Married by the Rev. Edward C. McGuire, Rector of St. George's Parish. Ministers' Returns.

2 November 1803. Charles F. GRETTER and Elizabeth Richards, dau. of John Richards. James Brown makes oath Elizabeth is over 21. Sur. William Cowan.

19 March 1833. Lewis GRIFFIN and Eliza Grigsby. Sur. Samuel B. Wilson.

7 December 1837. William GRIFFIN and Pamelia Lewis. Sur. Owen P. Foulke.

11 March 1843. Uriah GRIVES and Sarah Hall, dau. of Nancy Hall who consents. Sur. Henry Crowley.

31 July 1804. Daniel GRINNAN and Eliza Green of Spottsylvania Co. Sur. John Mundell.

16 September 1835. John GRINNAN and Elizabeth Jane Farish. Gincy Farish makes oath Elizabeth is over 21 but no relationship stated. Sur. George Alor.

31 April 1831. Henry W. GRINNAN and Jane Gaskins Crosley. Sur. David R. Donaldson.

17 January 1850. Robert A. GRINNAN and Robertine Temple. Sur. W. S. Barton.

17 December 1840. Charles GUTTRIDGE and Mary King. Sur. Arthur A. Jenkins who makes oath Mary is over 21.

13 February 1850. Charles GUTRIDGE and Elizabeth Bragdon. Sur. Arthur Jenkins.

26 December 1850. Leonard GUTRIDGE and Mary E. Cridlen. Sur. Jacob H. Cridlen.

8 March 1832. John W. HACKETT and Elizabeth Stevens. Sur. Michael Ames.

11 November 1844. Alphens HADLEY and Elizabeth Ashby. Sur. James Ashby.

13 January 1831. James HAGAN and Catherine Myers, dau. of Joshua Myers who consents. Sur. Turner H. Ramsey.

6 May 1847. John Henry HAILSTOCK and Louise Evans, dau. of Elizabeth Evans who consents. Sur. John Beckley.

23 November 1843. Charles C. HALL and Mary Elizabeth Anderson. Sur. George Cudlipp.

5 July 1848. Horace B. HALL and Alrerda C. Stuart. Sur. John B. Hall.

25 October 1817. John B. HALL and Harriet Stringfellow, dau. of Robert Stringfellow who is surety.

25 September 1845. Robert P. HALL and Charlotte Hall. Sur. Thomas J. Harrell.

10 May 1827. Hugh HAMILTON and Janet H. Scott. Sur. John Scott.

31 December 1839. William T. HANCOCK and Barbara McWhirt, dau. of Barbara McWhirt who consents. Sur. Robert A. Cox. Fredericksburg death records say William T. Hancock died 12 May 1858 aged 39. Son of William and Mary Hancock. Born in Orange Co. Wife, Barbara Hancock.

10 March 1837. William HANER and Ann Knight. Sur. James Mills who makes oath Ann is over 21.

11 May 1842. Thomas H. HANSON and Mary C. Parke. Sur. Reuben T. Thom.

19 June 1827. William HARDIA and Josephine Chismond. Sur. James B. Peake.

25 September 1849. James E. T. HARDIN and Ellen Frances Hogan. Sur. William W. Hogan. James E. T. Hardin son of William Hardin who writes consent.

14 October 1785. Benjamin HARRISON, Jr. and Anne Mercer. Sur. Thomas Brumfield.

23 May 1839. James HARRISON and Susan P. Helmistatter. Sur. John T. Baggott and James Cunningham.

2 May 1850. John W. HARRISON and Mary Frances Perry, dau. of James P. Perry who consents. Sur. Charles J. Curtis.

19 October 1815. Archibald HART and Ann Carmichael, dau. of James Carmichael who writes his consent. Sur. William Browne.

26 October 1843. Arthur R. HART and Evelina C. S. Goodwin. Sur. Arthur Goodwin.

16 October 1815. John HART and Harriet Green, dau. of Timothy Green. Sur. James Gallagher.

21 October 1835. John R. HART and Ann M. S. Goodwin. Sur. Charles Goodwin.

20 November 1832. Robert W. HART and Elizabeth W. Ellis. Sur. William E. Voss.

26 May 1824. William HARVEY and Maria Jones. Sur. John Ferneyhough who makes oath Maria is over 21.

20 February 1838. John HAYDON and Susan Colvert. Sur. John McShane who makes oath Susan is over 21.

22 February 1842. Patrick HAYDON and Martha Jane A. Taylor, dau. of Mary Taylor who consents. Sur. William T. Jones.

8 January 1846. John HAYWOOD and Martha Mills, dau. of Shady Mills. Sur. Owen Foulke.

3 December 1837. Henry H. HAZARD and Harriet A. Bibb. Sur. Thomas Bibb.

25 September 1838. Capt. Peter HAZLEGROVE and Jane Reveer, dau. of Julia Reveer who consents. Sur. Richard Wallace.

10 February 1810. Emanuel HEAD and Joice M. Jackson. Sur. William Caldwell.

11 April 1815. Alexander HENDERSON and Eliza Smith. Sur. Hugh M. Patton.

9 April 1838. Robert F. HENNING and Mildred Carter. Sur. Jeremiah Carter who makes oath Mildred is over 21.

31 May 1842. William D. HENRY and Julia A. Hall. Sur. John B. Hall.

31 July 1820. Jean Baptiste HERARD and Mary Ralls who writes her own consent. Sur. David Briggs. Of Jean Baptiste Herard a note says: "Born in France and dwelling in the city of Sens, department of Lyonne, being for a time in the United States of America".

21 April 1818. James HERNDON and Ann S. Estes, dau. of Triplett T. Estes who consents. Sur. Carter L. Stevenson.

18 April 1835. John M. HERNDON and Margaretta L. Patton. Sur. Brodie S. Herndon.

1 August 1844. William HEWLETT and Jane Dixon. Sur. William H. Bates who makes oath that both parties are over 21.

20 May 1844. Thomas K. HICKS and Virginia V. Green, dau. of William D. Green who is surety.

24 February 1849. Moses HILL and Matilda Gaines, "a free girl of colour". Sur. Joseph Russell. A note attached to the bond says "Matilda Gaines, a free woman of color wishes to marry Moses Hill. If the law allows it, Mr. Chew can issue the license. R. B. Semple."

3 January 1820. Titus H. HILL and Charlotte D. Matthews. Sur. Thomas Wright.

16 January 1811. James HILLDRUP and Jaley Carter. Sur. John H. C. Shepherd who makes oath both parties are over 21.

24 December 1833. Nathaniel HILLYARD and Jane W. Parks. Sur. Ro. B. Semple.

23 December 1834. Samuel J. HITCHCOCK and Narcissa P. Whittemore. Sur. Samuel B. Wilson.

16 October 1834. Frederick HOLDRIDGE and Catherine Elizabeth Burton. Sur. James Holmes.

28 March 1818. Thomas S. HOLLOWAY and Ann M. Crump. Sur. John Crump.

4 November 1840. Hay B. HOOMES and Eleanor E. Johnston. Sur. Malcalm H. Crump.

28 December 1841. Albert HOOTON and Isabella M. Johnson, dau. of Jane Johnson who consents. Sur. George Cudlipp.

22 October 1845. Albert HOOTON and Mary Jane Rose. Sur. William Pritchard.

21 Septembr 1824. Peter HORD and Harriet Benson. Sur. George Baggott.

23 December 1819. William HORTON and Harriet E. Martin, widow. Sur. Thompson Schooler.

2 November 1835. John D. HOUSTON and Martha H. Wilson. Sur. Samuel B. Wilson.

13 November 1850. Samuel S. Howison and Ann Eliza Ficklen, dau. of Catherine Ficklen who consents. Sur. J. Warren Slaughter.

30 April 1828. Robert HUGDIN and Sarah R. Graham. Sur. William F. Gray.

27 May 1840. Landon J. HUFFMAN and Ann Proctor, dau. of Mary Proctor who consents. Sur. George F. Chew.

21 April 1845. John HULL and Ann Eliza Crump. Sur. William T. Hart.

1 September 1832. Conrad H. HUNT and Elizabeth S. Drinnan. Sur. William B. Peake.

21 December 1833. Gilbert J. HUNT and Jane Jones. Sur. George Alor.

26 August 1786. Benjamin HYDE and Mary Young. Sur. Henry Armistead.

7 November 1839. Taliaferro HUNTER and Lucy Ann Tennant. Sur. John James Chew.

13 May 1813. Valentine INGRAM and Nancy Williams. Sur. William J. Williams.

8 December 1821. Caesar JACKSON and Rosetta Cole. Sur. John Sexsmith. Contracting parties "Free Persons of colour".

3 May 1786. John JACKSON and Elizabeth Caldwell. Sur. Phillip Evans.

8 November 1813. Samuel JACKSON and Maria Lewis. Sur. Nancy Lewis. Contracting parties "Free persons of colour".

29 February 1848. Walter JACKSON and Ann Eliza Lewis. Sur. Ryland Rives.

6 February 1838. William A. JACKSON and Sarah Ann Hillyard. Sur. Benjamin R. Hillyard.

9 May 1820. Charles P. JAMES and Eliza Cooke. Sur. James Cooke.

24 July 1806. John JAMES and Nancy Patterson. Sur. John Rogers.

30 May 1836. John H. JAMES and Mary Wilson Crawford, dau. of George Crawford who writes consent. Sur. Edward McDowell.

23 May 1831. Francis D. JARVIS and Sarah Jane Ames. Sur. Michael Ames and Joshua Myers.

8 March 1832. Thomas JEFFERSON and Mary Toombs. Sur. John James Chew.

5 October 1848. William J. JEFFRIES and Mary E. Tate. Sur. Charles W. Gore who makes oath Mary is over 21.

27 November 1841. Arthur JENKINS and Fenton Garner. Sur. Robert Garner who makes oath Fenton is over 21.

11 November 1840. James JENKINS and Elizabeth Betty. Sur. Gilford Edrington who makes oath Elizabeth is over 21.

22 August 1849. James JENKINS and Rosey Guthrie. Sur. William True who makes oath Rosey is over 21.

25 December 1844. Robert JENKINS and Susan Ann Barnes. Sur. Benjamin Eskridge who makes oath both parties are over 21.

9 September 1835. George JENNINGS and Susan Portch, dau. of Pieshous Portch who consents. Sur. Thomas Jennings and William L. Chandler.

28 March 1820. James JENNINGS and Nancy Girgsby Grady. Sur. Thomas Wren.

7 November 1850. James JENNINGS and Lucretia Long, dau. of Martha Long who consents. Sur. Jacob Schaut.

30 November 1848. William JENNINGS and Catharine Curtis. Sur. James Jennings who makes oath Catharine is over 21.

5 April 1838. William P. JESSE and Emily Lyon. Sur. James Williams who makes oath Emily is over 21.

31 December 1831. George JETT and Mary Rese. Sur. George Limbrick who makes that Mary Rese is his daughter (step-daughter?) and "upwards of 21".

28 October 1850. James H. JETT and Mrs. Mary Bridwell. Sur. James A. Turner.

7 September 1849. William JETT and Sarah Jane Dunnevant, dau. of Hezekiah Dunnevant who is surety, consents and makes oath Sarah Jane is over 21.

13 May 1843. Benjamin JOHNSON and Henrietta Ferguson, dau. of James Ferguson who is surety and makes oath Henrietta is over 21. Polly Curtis makes oath Benjamin Johnson is over 21. George Latham also makes oath he has known Benjamin Johnson (a man of color) for many years and that he is over 21. Contracting parties "Free persons of colour".

18 July 1819. Littleton D. JOHNSON and Jane Cooley. Sur. Timothy Green.

17 August 1825. John JOHNSON and Maria Lewis. Sur. John Liverpool.

31 January 1837. Richard L. JOHNSON and Mary Somerville Powell, dau. of Elizabeth Powell who consents. Sur. James Harris.

28 April 1804. Charles Smith JOHNSTON and Lucy Victor, dau. of John Victor who consents. Sur. Richard Johnston.

28 March 1816. Fayette JOHNSTON and Eliza Pearson, dau. of William Pearson who is surety.

13 September 1832. Gabriel JOHNSTON and Adelaid C. Barnett, dau. of Benjamin N. Barnett who consents. Sur. Charles A. Pearson.

17 May 1806. James JOHNSTON and Eleanor Evans. Sur. James Newby.

28 November 1831. James R. JOHNSTON and Mary T. Nicholson. Sur. Robert H. Crump. Bond signed James R. Johnson.

28 March 1820. Larkin JOHNSTON and Julia Pearson, dau. of William Pearson who is surety.

10 August 1805. Richard JOHNSTON and Ann M. Dare. Sure. Burkett Bowen.

3 September 1811. Richard JOHNSTON, Jr. and Anna Maria Heiskell. Horace Marshall, guardian of Anna, consents and is surety. An attached note says: "This is to certify that Richard Johnston, Jr. and Ann Maria Heiskell was married on the 5th of September 1811 William James."

13 August 1832. William JOHNSTON and Alice Stern. Sur. James Wilkins. Minister's returns say Alice Sterns. Bond signed William Johnson.

14 July 1827. Charles F. JONES and Sophia Stiple. Sur. Thomas S. Clarke.

3 April 1805. George JONES and Elizabeth Green. Sur. James Bates who makes oath Elizabeth is 21 & upwards.

1 December 1836. Henry JONES and Jane Jett. Sur. Lemuel Thompson who makes oath Jane is over 21.

1 October 1849. James C. JONES and Ophelia Layton, dau. of Robert G. Layton who consents. Sur. James Raines.

8 March 1830. James R. JONES and Mary King. Sur. Thomas Calvert who makes oath Mary is over 21.

5 January 1843. John L. JONES and Martha Short. Sur. William U. Short who makes oath John L. Jones is 21.

14 November 1849. John W. JONES and Eliza Byram. Sur. O. H. Reamy who makes oath both parties over 21.

24 March 1787. Thomas JONES and Elizabeth Frye. Sur. James Slayter.

29 September 1810. William JONES and Lucy Peters. Sur. James Ferguson. Contracting parties "Free people of colour".

10 August 1815. William JONES and Rebecca Grady, age 31. Sur. Anthony Rawlins.

29 March 1838. William L. JONES AND Lucy Ann Baggott. Sur. George Baggott who makes oath William L. Jones is over 21.

22 May 1850. William Strother JONES and Mary Eliza Barton. Sur. William S. Barton.

4 September 1839. William T. JONES and Frances E. L. Daniel. Sur. William U. Short who makes oath Frances is over 21.

19 May 1823. Isham JORDON and Matilda Randall. Sur. Samuel Knowles. Ann Jett makes oath that Matilda Randall lives with her in Fredericksburg, that she is an orphan without guardian and is over 21.

20 December 1842. Christian J. KAUFFMAN and Susan A. White. Sur. Jesse White.

29 September 1844. John KELLY and Selina L. Wrenn, dau. of Thomas Wrenn of Spottsylvania Co. Sur. George F. Chew.

23 September 1824. Perry KELLY and Ann Cunningham. Sur. James Cunningham.

8 April 1846. William KEMEYS and Ann F. L. Carmichael. Sur. Edward H. Carmichael.

25 January 1848. James T. KENDALL and Mary E. Gaskins, dau. of Mary Gaskins who consents. Sur. James Walker. James T. Kendall son of Henrietta H. Browne who consents.

28 December 1841. Horace S. KIMBALL and Mahala Ann Wrenn, dau. of Melinda T. Wrenn who consents. Sur. B. B. Thyer.

18 October 1843. George H. KING and Mary Jefferson (widow). Sur. William Jones.

19 August 1845. George P. KING and Susan Warren, dau. of William Warren who consents. Sur. James P. Whaling.

20 June 1839. James B. KING and Sarah Ann Dabney. Sur. Horace Clarke.

18 July 1840. John B. KING and Mary L. Williams. Sur. James L. Williams.

4 January 1833. William KING and Eloise M. King. Sur. Isaac M. King.

6 October 1849. Charles F. KIRK and Betty M. Byram, dau. of John Byram. Sur. Robert A. Nelson.

30 April 1808. John Ellis KNIGHT and Agnes Poole, dau. of Frances Poole who consents. Sur. James Lyon who makes oath Agnes' Father is dead and Frances Poole is her Mother.

7 April 1830. John Lunsford Lomax KNIGHT and Ellen Mattison. Sur. Lewis Burke. Deed Bk. I p. 393 records the marriage contract.

3 October 1816. John S. KNOX and Elizabeth A. Seldon. Married by the Rev. Edward C. McGuire, Rector of St. George's Parish. Ministers' Returns.

2 February 1804. William LANPHIER and Mary Sexsmith. Sur. Simon Sexsmith. The name is signed William Lanphier on the bond but seemingly spelled Lamphier in the same document.

20 August 1785. John LAWRENCE and Elizabeth Mead who writes own consent. Sur. John Hall.

3 August 1846. Catlett LAWSON and Fanny Armstrong. Sur. Arthur Jenkins who makes oath Fanny is over 21.

16 January 1822. Fielding LAWSON and Elizabeth Daniel. Sur. William Jones who makes oath both parties over 21.

12 October 1832. James LAWSON and Maria West. Sur. Adolph Richards.

30 October 1832. Nathaniel LAWSON and Emily Burnett. Sur. John Layton. Attached to the bond is this note: This is to certify that I am 21 years of age October 31st, 1832, Emily Barnet.

15 February 1843. Charles LAYTON and Georgiana Perry. Sur. James Jenkins who makes oath both parties over 21.

29 November 1830. John LAYTON and Cassandra Porter. Sur. Robert G. Layton.

17 January 1825. Robert G. LAYTON and Pheba Holbrook. Sur. Horace Clark. Fanny Holbrook makes oath her younger sister Phebe is over 21.

26 December 1850. William LAYTON and Rebecca Frances Layton. Sur. Robert G. Layton.

21 December 1804. Michael LEA and Mary Steigar. Sur. John Steigar.

10 May 1849. William T. LEAGUE and Francis Ann Bradshaw. Sur. Uriah H. Bradshaw.

7 December 1808. John LEAR and Alice Doggett. Sur. Alexander Walker.

5 February 1822. Albert LEE and Eliza Hooten. Sur. Peter P. Cox. "Margaret Hooten, mother of Eliza Hooten makes oath the said Eliza is 21. William F. Phillips Deputy Clerk of said Court."

12 August 1819. Hancock LEE and Susan Ann Richards, ward of George B. Richards who is surety.

13 April 1804. Lewis LEE and Sally Johnson. Sur. John Hall.

16 September 1820. Pierre Henry LEUBA and Claude Victorine Herard. Sur. Jean Baptiste Herard.

25 November 1847. Henry LEVY and Sarah Leach, dau. of Patsy Leach who consents. Sur. Uriah H. Bradshaw.

23 December 1840. Charles H. LEWIS and Ellen T. Lomax. Sur. Gerard B. Stuart.

27 November 1834. George LEWIS and Ann Truslow. Sur. Jeremiah Allen.

11 December 1784. Henry LEWIS and Cytha Brown. Sur. Thomas Brown.

14 August 1817. James LEWIS and Elizabeth Duncan, dau. of Alexander Duncan who consents. Sur. Sthreshley Simmons.

15 November 1820. James LEWIS and Milly Webb. Sur. John Evans. Contracting parties "Free persons of colour."

20 May 1836. James LEWIS and Maria Butler. Sur. David Rose who makes oath both are upwards of 21.

9 May 1840. James LEWIS and Ann Micou. Sur. Hiram Perry who makes oath Ann is over 21.

27 May 1809. John LEWIS and Mildred A. B. Mercer. Sur. Warner W. Lewis.

15 September 1840. John E. LEWIS and Mary M. Drinan. Sur. Conrad H. Hunt.

14 September 1842. Samuel H. LEWIS and Ann Maria Lomax. Sur. John T. Lomax, Jr.

17 December 1844. Washington LEWIS and Harriet Robey, widow, "who usually resides in Fredericksburg". Sur. Richard Bowling.

10 September 1811. William LEWIS and Lydia Grant. Sur. John Murphey who makes oath both are over 21. "This is to certify that William Lewis and Lydia Grant was married on the 10th of September 1811. William James."

14 June 1820. William LEWIS and Husley Hollinger. Sur. Edmund Hollinger. Contracting parties "Free persons of colour."

9 September 1847. William LEWIS and Henrietta Evans. Sur. John S. G. Timberlake.

13 April 1841. John LEYBURN and Mary Louise Stuart Mercer, dau. of Hugh Mercer who consents. Sur. Robert A. Grinnan.

18 June 1838. Philip L. LIGHTFOOT and Mary Virginia Smith. Her only surviving parent, Delia Smith writes her consent. Sur. Robert G. Robb.

3 December 1838. Dickinson LILLY and Suckey Jackson, alias Suckey Chambers. Sur. London Lilly.

18 November 1833. London LILLY and Emily Lewis Montague. Sur. Robert S. Chew.

13 March 1813. William H. LILLY and Elizabeth Brown, dau. of Charles Brown, deceased, of Fredericksburg. The following paper is with this bond: "We, John Robinson and Nancy Robinson, wife of the said John, formerly Nancy Brown, widow of Charles Brown, deceased, do hereby certify that Elizabeth Brown, daughter of the said Nancy has no guardian chosen by herself or appointed by any court and we are the natural guardians of the said Elizabeth do hereby direct the Clerk of the Corp. Court of Fredg. to issue a license for the marriage of the said Elizabeth to William H. Lilly of Fredericksburg. Witness our hands this 13th March 1813. John Robinson, Nancy Robinson."

14 April 1819. Jesse LIPSCOMB and Susan H. Dabney, widow, who writes own consent. Sur. Ambrose Watkins, who makes oath Jesse Lipscomb is over 21.

20 December 1826. Isaac LIVERPOOL and Eliza Johnson. Sur. John Liverpool who makes oath both are over 21.

29 September 1824. John LIVERPOOL and Ann Johnston. Sur. Henry Moore.

22 July 1805. John Tayloe LOMAX and Charlotte Belson Thornton, dau. of Presly Thornton of the State of New York who writes his consent dating same 4 May 1805. Wit. John Fitzhugh and William Helm. Sur. John Minor.

27 May 1844. P. Thornton LOMAX and Mildred Henderson Wellford, dau. of John S. Wellford who consents. Sur. John James Chew.

10 February 1803. Thomas Lunsford LOMAX and Martha Johnston. Sur. Richard Johnston.

29 January 1834. Benjamin LONG and Maria Louisa Kale, dau. of Anthony Kale who consents. Sur. Robert Parrott.

1 June 1831. George M. LONG and Rebecca C. Lucas. Sur. Thomas W. Gray.

21 May 1818. James LONG and Patsy Clark, dau. of Charles Clark who is surety.

17 December 1822. Lunsford H. LONG and Ann Lucas, dau. of Fielding Lucas who is surety.

29 December 1803. Thomas Edward LORD and Anna Stribling, dau. of Samuel Stribling who is surety.

14 November 1821. Francis LOWERY and Susan Jane Chapman, ward of said Francis Lowry. Sur. Thomas Curtis. The name is spelled Lowery and Lowry interchangeably in the bond: signed Francis Lowery.

31 October 1848. James LUCAS and Eliza Vass. Sur. Jacob Nicholas. Contracting parties "Free persons of colour".

12 February 1850. William LUCAS and Ann Frazer. Sur. James Lucas.

5 October 1827. Willis LUCAS and Jemimah West. Sur. Isaac Liverpool who makes oath both are over 21.

19 April 1783. Zachariah LUCAS and Polly Harrison Apperson, dau. of John Apperson consent only, no bond has been found. The following letter is filed with the marriage bonds for the letter L: "Sir: You will please grant a license to Mr. Zachariah Lucas for a marriage intended to be had and soleminized between him the said Mr. Zachariah Lucas and my daughter Polly Harrison Apperson. Given under my hand and seal this 19th day of April 1785. John Apperson (seals). To Henry Armistead, Clerk of the Hustings Court of Fredericksburg.

24 March 1836. James LUNSFORD and Margaret English. Sur. Michael Ames who makes oath Margaret is over 21.

7 October 1747. Samuel LYELL and Sarah Wiatt. Married by the Rev. Edward C. McGuire, Rector of St. George's Parish. Ministers' Returns.

14 October 1841. Micajah T. LYNCH and Virginia Lorimer. Sur. John James Chew.

23 August 1825. William LYONS and Dorothea Harrod. Sur. George F. Chew, consent of Rebecca T. Lomax, no relationship stated, who makes oath Dorothea is 21.

24 September 1839. Charles McCALLEY and Mary Head. Sur. William S. Chesley.

17 May 1848. Francis G. McCALLEY and Hellen W. Anderson, dau. of M. D. Anderson who consents. Sur. Lewis O. Magrath.

9 October 1823. William McDANIEL and Mary Huggins. Charles Austin guardian of Mary, is surety.

17 November 1829. William McDANIEL and Frances J. Bertier. Sur. John Roy.

22 July 1846. Mathew McDOUGAL and Elizabeth Cavanaugh. Sur. James Collins and Mathew Lyons.

8 December 1828. Edward McDOWELL and Maria Ann Smith. George Crawford guardian of Maria Ann consents. Sur. Benjamin Long.

3 May 1786. John McFARLIN and Margaret Swinney. Sur. Richard Kenney. Note: Surname of bride is very indistinct.

26 May 1835. Alexander McGEE and Rebecca Jones. Sur. William Rose.

6 December 1837. Thomas John McGILL and Julia A. Phillips. Sur. Alexander K. Phillips.

17 April 1816. Rev. Edward C(harles) McGUIRE and Judith C(arter) Lewis, dau. of Robert Lewis who consents. Sur. William A. Knox. Edward Charles McGuire b. 26 July 1793 Frederick Co. Va. d. 8 Oct. 1858 Fredericksburg, Va. Rector St. George's Parish 1813-1858. Judith Carter Lewis, dau. Robert Lewis and Judith Brown; grand dau. Col. Fielding Lewis and his 2nd wife Betty Washington sister of Gen. George Washington. She was b. 4 Oct. 1794 d. 26 Mar. 1882. Dates from tombstones.

11 November 1840. James McGUIRE and Jane Elizabeth Ellis. Sur. Robert W. Hart.

6 November 1833. John H. McGUIRE and Anne F. Fitzhugh. Sur. John J. Chew.

19 January 1847. Thomas McHENRY and Helen Virginia Jennings. Sur. S. J. Haupt.

29 May 1816. Gerard McKENNEY and Elizabeth Whitehead, widow. Sur. Robert S. Chew.

13 February 1823. Jesse G. McKENNEY and Mary Ann Ridley, ward of Reubin T. Thom who is surety.

20 June 1809. William McKENNY and Hannah Spencer. Seth Spencer consents, no relationship stated. Sur. George Nicholson. William McKenny of Culpeper County.

8 July 1833. Samuel McKENZIE and Patsy Wright. Sur. George Cox.

14 November 1840. George McLEOD and Jane Meredith. Sur. John Eubank.

15 November 1843. George McLEOD and Mary Ann McFarlane. Sur. Alexander A. Muse.

18 February 1837. John McSHANE and Ann Elizabeth Newton. Sur. Thomas Howard.

30 January 1786. Joshua McWILLIAMS and Mary Blythe. Sur. John Skinker.

6 January 1812. Robert MACKAY and Maria Fisher. Sur. Donald Campbell.

6 March 1817. Robert MACABOY and Sucky Magee. Sur. Thompson Nailer.

22 November 1831. John H. MADDOX and Frances S. Young. Sur. William B. Ross.

2 December 1830. William MADDOX and Mary Ann Curtis. Sur. James Curtis.

9 March 1831. Francis MADOWNY and Rosa Ann Berry. Sur. James West. Mary Ann Clark makes oath Rosa is 21. Contracting parties "Free persons of colour". This paper accompanies the bond: "I hereby certify that Rosa Ann Berry a bright mulatto girl now living with me is 21 years old, she having been bannd to me and served her time and lived with me ever since. Given under my hand and seal this 9th day of March 1831. Mary Ann Clark." Married by the Rev. Edward C. McGuire.

26 June 1834. James MANDOWNEY and Patsey Jackson. Sur. Willis Lucas.

5 July 1838. Henry MANN and Alice Tascoe. Sur. Joseph Mann.

30 December 1839. Thomas MANUELL and Mary Ann Wood, dau. of Tomzin Wood who consents. Sur. Landon J. Huffman.

30 July 1850. Levi D. MARCHANT and Henrietta Wroughton. Sur. Moris Montgomery.

5 September 1805. Horace MARSHALL and Elizabeth Heiskell. Sur. John Stanard.

15 February 1831. Hugh R. MARSHALL and Ann Maria Crissey. Sur. Samuel Runyon.

6 July 1820. Francis MARTIN and Lucy Ellis. Married by the Rev. Edward C. McGuire, Rector of St. George's Parish. Ministers' Returns.

29 October 1846. John L. MARYE, Jr. and Milly Stone Browne. Sur. Charles Herndon.

8 June 1848. William J. (or F.) MASSEY and Jane Walker. Sur. William F. Walker.

19 January 1804. Mordecai MASTIN and Lucy Bennett. Sur. Jacob Grotz.

23 September 1812. John MAURY and Patty Allen, ward of Garrit Minor who is surety.

25 June 1803. Philip MAYER and Jane McFarlane. Sur. Stephen McFarlane.

10 March 1836. Dr. John MAYO and Sarah S. Tennent. Sur. Benjamin F. Taliaferro.

27 January 1838. James MAZEEN and Mary Ann Keeton. Sur. John M. Keeton.

19 December 1815. Richard K. MEADE and Rebecca S. Green, dau. of Timothy Green who is surety.

23 November 1810. John METCALFE and Catharine Johnson. Sur. William A. Gregory.

18 November 1836. John H. MICOU and Ann Johnson. Sur. James Suthard.

4 September 1820. Henry O. MIDDLETON and Mildred E. Crutchfield. Sur. Beverley R. Wellford.

4 January 1841. Gibson Z. MILES and Catharine B. Wood, dau. of Tomzin Wood who consents. Sur. Robert A. Cox.

23 May 1842. George MILLER and Lucy A. Parrish. Sur. John G. Parrish.

6 October 1840. Henry MILLER and Sarah Peyton. Sur. John Timberlake.

29 September 1813. John MILLER and Patsy Williams. Sur. William L. Lewis. In the presence of John Snow and Thomas Crosley. Helhy (?) Williams makes oath her daughter Patsy is 36.

11 December 1850. Joseph R. MILLER and Lucy Ellen Graves, dau. of Harriet Graves who consents. Sur. Anthony Brackett.

5 July 1837. Charles C. MILLS and Catharine A. King. Sur. John James Chew.

22 February 1836. Francis S. MILLS and Catharine White. Sur. Jesse White.

13 July 1847. James H. MILLS and Harriet O. Shelton. Sur. W. S. Briggs.

6 January 1840. James T. MILLS and Elizabeth Mullen, dau. of Charles Mullen who is surety.

13 May 1816. Robert MILLS and Eliza Burden, dau. of Archibald Burden who is surety. Robert Mills son of Elizabeth Mills who states he was born 21 July 1794.

6 December 1838. Robert T. MILLS and Maria Browne. Sur. William B. Hore and Lindsey Pullen.

15 September 1819. Thomas P. MILLS and Joanna Jones, ward of Charles Jones who is surety.

27 October 1841. Walter M. MILLS and Pamelia Perry. Sur. William B. Hore.

17 May 1826. William MILUS and Shady Puzey, ward of William Milus. Sur. Robert S. Chew.

12 September 1848. Wheeler MINNIS and Lucy Ann Pullen. Sur. William Quisenberry.

6 August 1840. George MINOR and Ann Eliza Chew. Sur. Geroge F. Chew. George Minor born 1808, died 1879. Ann Eliza Chew born 1809, died 1898. Dates from Fredericksburg City Cemetery tombstones.

10 December 1839. William G. MINOR and Ann F. Rootes. Sur. George F. Carmichael.

7 March 1786. Thomas MOFFATT, Gentleman, and Anne Maria Mortimer, dau. of Dr. Charles Mortimer who consents. Sur. Thomas Brumfield.

11 August 1824. Henry MOOR and Lucinda Duncan. Sur. John Liverpool.

3 October 1844. Edward MOORE and Elizabeth Parke. Sur. William J. Walker.

12 June 1827. John MOORE and Susan Jones. Sur. Stiles P. Curtis.

8 May 1850. John Conway MONCURE and Fanny Dulany Tomlin. Sur. Eustace Conway.

21 June 1849. Edward MONDOWNEY and Lucy Keyes, dau. of Maria Keys. Sur. Henry Bird.

6 March 1848. James MONDOWNEY and Jane Green. Sur. Robert Stephens.

30 October 1838. Edwin R. MORGAN and Eliza Purks. Sur. Enoch Rollins.

31 October 1843. James A. MORGAN and Eliza Cudlipp. Sur. Albert Hooten.

20 September 1821. Alexander MORRIS and Sophia R. Spilman, dau. of Peter Spilman who is surety.

25 March 1847. James F. MORRIS and Mary Ann Elizabeth Wiltshire, dau. of Benjamin Wiltshire who is surety with Frederick Powell.

31 July 1849. Dr. Edwin A MORRISON and Lucia B. Hackley, dau. of M. Hackley who consents. Sur. R. J. Morrison.

19 July 1845. William N. MORRISON and Susan Limbrick, widow. Sur. Edward Stone.

18 September 1832. Alexander MORSON and Maria M. Berry. Sur. Arthur A. Morson.

5 May 1803. John MORTIMER and Mary French. Sur. George French.

8 November 1827. Allen W. MORTON and Jean Mitchell. Sur. John J. Chew.

31 December 1822. Caleb MULLEN and Sarah Sindall, dau. of William and Judey Sindall of Fredericksburg who consent. Sur. Edward Sindall.

15 December 1847. Charles MULLEN and Mary Pitman. Sur. Lewis Burke.

18 October 1838. James MULLEN and Olivia Barnes. Sur. John Sterling.

1 December 1828. Ryland MULLEN and Ann Curtis. Sur. Thomas Calvert and Alexander Beech.

5 March 1844. Ryland MULLEN and Susan Burden. Sur. James C. Wright.

17 December 1849. George MULLIN (MULLEN) and Virginia E. Towles. Sur. Henry M. Towles. This name spelled both ways in the bond, but he signs Mullin.

20 August 1838. Nicholas MULVAY and Betsy Lewis. Sur. Edward McAdams. Married by the Rev. Edward C. McGuire, Rector of St. George's Parish.

7 January 1828. John MUNDILL and Jennette McIntosh. Sur. Peter Goolrick. E. Grinnan consents without indicating relationship with either party. The name is spelled Mundill and Mundell, but he signs Mundill.

5 October 1816. James MURPHEY and Mary Burnett. Sur. Alexander Walker.

3 June 1811. John MURPHY and Leanah Grady. Sur. Samuel McKenzie.

20 November 1845. Alexander MURRAY and Martha A. Layton. Sur. William Pritchard.

27 April 1811. Ebenezer MURRAY and Elizabeth Saunders. Sur. William Jackson.

17 September 1839. William MURRAY and Elizabeth Waite, dau. of Jesse Wayt, who consents. Sur. Robert A. Cox.

19 January 1826. William Thompson MURREN and Mary McPherson, ward of Benjamin Clark who is surety.

8 April 1830. Alexander Alfred MUSE and Catharine Mayers. Sur. John Minor.

23 December 1834. John MYERS and Catharine Hagan. Sur. E. Lucas.

30 April 1811. Joshua MYERS, Jr. and Sarah Ann Pope. Sur. William Pope. Joshua Myers of Spottsylvania County, father of Joshua Myers, Jr., gives his consent.

26 September 1804. Jesse NALLE and Nancy Botts. Sur. Benjamin Botts.

10 July 1817. Armistead NELSON and Mary Henderson, dau. of David Henderson. Sur. John S. Wellford.

7 September 1848. Robert A. NELSON and Mary Byram. Sur. Frederick Powell.

16 July 1849. William Meade NELSON and Sarah Wilhemina Semmes. Sur. John M. Forbes.

12 November 1818. James W. NEWBY and Jane Phoebe White, dau. of Henry White who is surety.

11 July 1832. William NEWMAN and Leydia Anderson Neberker. Sur. Hezekiah Best and John Sterling.

17 October 1786. John NEWTON, Jr. and Judith Pollard. Sur. Pirtchard
Newby. This letter accompanies the bond: "Dear Johnny: Your brother
Benney informd me that you are going b be marryed to Miss Pollard and
desire to know whether I am willing that it should be so. I have
nothing to say about the matter please yourself child and you wont
offend me nor your Mother either. I always shall be glad to see you
and your wife. From your Loving father 'till death, John Newton, Senr.
October 12, 1786; To Mr. John Newton.

13 September 1843. Edgar NICHOLS and Lucy Ann Clarke, dau. of Almira
Jenkins who consents. Sur. Gilbert Edrington.

23 November 1850. George L. NICHOLSON and Bettie B. Wellford. Sur.
Armistead N. Wellford.

11 March 1812. John NOBLE and Elizabeth Griffin. Sur. John Thompson,
Sheriff. Elizabeth makes oath she is over 21 and that she has neither
father nor mother living. John Noble is described as a "bookbinder of
Fredericksburg."

25 April 1820. Flavius S. NOEL and Anna Pearson. Sur. James Cooke.

24 September 1846. Benjamin W. NORTON and Elizabeth Clarke. Sur.
Charles Layton.

11 January 1806. George NORWOOD and Mrs. Ann Ingham, dau. of Mrs.
Eleanor Welch. Sur. George Welch. See Culpeper County Chancery Paper,
Box #9 in suit Norwood vs. Strother.

20 January 1848. Peter NOSSETT and Catharine Aldridge. Sur. Roy Jones.

3 August 1812. William ORILL and Elizabeth West. Sur. William Wines
and Thomas Dodson. The following unsigned statement accompanies this
bond: "Elizabeth West was born on the 11th day of February 1787. She
is therefore 24 years of age the 11th day of last February 1811".

16 April 1831. Sidney H. OWENS and Jane E. Beck. Sur. George Cox.

24 April 1806. Mann PAGE and Mary W. Lithgow. Sur. Charles L. Carter.

5 February 1817. Jeremiah PARISH and Mary Ann Clarke, widow. Sur.
George Fry.

4 December 1839. John G. PARISH and Elizabeth S. Bunberry. Sur.
William S. Chesley. Robert L. Blackburne makes oath Elizabeth is over
21.

17 June 1817. Lewis PARRISH and Elizabeth Whiting, widow of John Whiting. Sur. Vivian Ashby. The following accompanies this bond: "Mr.
Robert S. Chew, Sir: You are hereby authorized and requested to issue
license to unite in marriage my daughter Mrs. Elizabeth Whiter (widow

(continued)

of John Whiter, deceased) to Lewis Parrish and this shall be your security for the same. Lawrence L. Boores, Catherine Boores". Fred'g. 17th June 1817. Elizabeth Whiting, nee Scags, was stepdau. of Lawrence L. Boores.

20 June 1844. Edward PARKER and Sarah Wood. Sur. Henry Young.

27 March 1833. John PARROTT, Jr, and Susan E. Parrott, dau of Robert Parrott who consents. Sur. Robert Parrott, Jr.

12 April 1836. Robert PARROTT and Ann E. Parrott. Sur. George W. Parrott.

8 January 1824. John M. PATTON and Peggy F. S. Williams. Sur. Isaac H. Williams.

31 August 1835. William Farley PATTON and Harriet S. Buck. Sur. John J. Chew.

10 July 1837. A. M. PAXTON and Mary L. Ellis, dau. of Robert Ellis who consents. Sur. Robert W. Hart.

13 February 1850. Elzey PAYNE and Catharine Fries. Sur. Jacob Fries and Daniel Payne.

16 July 1839. Joshua A. PAYNE and Elizabeth W. Phillips. Sur. Charles Gutridge.

30 April 1782. Capt. William PENNOCK and Ann Tucker who writes her own consent. Sur. Peter Minor.

6 October 1841. Abner PERKINS and Asinath Merrill. Sur. Octavius Reany.

20 October 1819. Austin PERRY and Emily Milna. Sur. Thomas Wright.

13 March 1839. Elisha PERRY and Juliet Ann Jenkins. Sur. Peter Hazlegrove.

9 December 1834. Hiram PERRY and Mary Southard. Sur. James Southard.

4 November 1847. Joseph W. PERRY and Margaret Ingram. Sur. George Alor.

5 March 1829. Alexander PEYTON and Mary Snipe. Sur. James Peyton.

4 May 1850. Alexander PEYTON and Elizabeth Davis. Sur. John J. Chew and William Warren, Jr.

23 November 1843. Charles C. PEYTON and Mary Ann Gutridge. Sur. Joel R. Jenkins.

31 March 1847. George Henry PEYTON and Lucy Barrett. Sur. John Toombs who makes oath that V. Peyton father of George Henry Peyton has been absent from Virginia for seven or eight years and is supposed to be dead. His mother gives consent and signs her name Ann Sacrey.

6 July 1816. Henry PHILEUM and Isabella McIntosh. Sur. John Mundell.

7 February 1810. John PHILLIPS and Lucinda Reeves, dau. of Mary Reeves who gives her consent. Sur. Samuel Jones.

3 January 1811. John T. PHILLIPS and Lucinda Reeves, dau. of Mary Reeves who consents. Sur. Samuel McKenzie.

11 November 1835. Richard H. PHILLIPS and Eleanor Thom. Sur. Alexander K. Phillips.

20 December 1838. Shelton PHILLIPS and Ellen Massey. Sur. Battle Massey.

17 October 1849. George W. PICKETT and Mary Jane True, dau. of Alolphus True who consents. Sur. George W. Wroten.

26 July 1833. Jeremiah PICKETT and Elizabeth Solivan. Sur. David R. Donaldson.

23 October 1828. Hiram PILCHER and Mary A. Beck, dau. of Elizabeth Beck who certifies her daughter is 21. Sur. John S. Caldwell.

17 April 1839. Robert PINN and Elizabeth Jackson. Sur. William Lewis.

20 March 1849. William Henry PIPER and Sarah West. Sur. Aleysius Baggett.

5 June 1844. David A. PITMAN and Nancy Grotz, dau. of John Grotz who is surety.

13 June 1850. John F. PITTMAN and Caroline M. Muse. Sur. Alexander A. Muse who makes oath both are upwards of 21.

30 January 1838. John W. PITTMAN and Betty Grotz. Sur. John Grotz.

7 December 1803. Joseph POLLARD and Susannah Peacock, dau. of Richard Peacock who consents. Sur. Henry White.

20 August 1849. George POLLETT and Mildred Daingerfield. Sur. Samuel Lyell.

29 October 1803. Thomas S. POPE and Sarah Flack, whose "next friend" is William James who is surety.

31 July 1823. John PORTER and Casandra Thompson. Sur. Lemuel Thompson.

13 November 1807. Timothy POTTS and Catharine Curran. Sur. James Trammell.

11 October 1848. Richard POWELL and Ellin Elkins. Sur. Elijah Bowling.

10 February 1826. John PREBLE and Nancy Bancroft. Sur. Lindsey Pullen. John Preble described as "Mariner of Fredericksburg".

7 February 1844. Lewis M. PREVOST and Laura E. McCarty. Sur. P. Thornton Lomax.

7 November 1806. Edward PRITCHARD and Mary Brown, dau. of James Brown. Married by the Rev. S. B. Wilson. Ministers' Returns.

15 August 1839. John PRITCHARD and Harriet S. Barnett. Sur. James B. Timberlake.

19 July 1833. Charles PROCTER and Maria Trainer. Sur. Thomas Lewis.

26 December 1815. Thomas PROCTOR and Christiana Keys, widow. Sur. Robert S. Chew.

14 March 1844. Thomas PROCTOR and Eleanor Snellings, dau. of Elizabeth Snellings. Sur. James Curtis.

5 April 1847. Thomas PROCTOR and Sarah Heslep. Sur. William A. Heslep.

14 March 1850. Edwin R. PULLEN and Elizabeth Sibley, ward of Capt. E. E. Rollins. Sur. Enoch E. Rollins.

2 May 1828. Jesse PULLEN and Eliza Shepherd, dau. and ward of Lucy Shepherd. Sur. Henry T. Phillips.

5 March 1834. Jesse PULLEN and Lucy M. Ames. Sur. Michael Ames.

21 December 1831. John QUARLES and Sarah Daniel. Sur. Thomas Daniel.

1 May 1821. William QUESENBERRY and Frances Davis, widow. Sur. Thompson Schooler.

21 December 1848. Libern P. RAINES and Caroline H. Kersey. Sur. Abraham Cox.

16 August 1814. James RANALDSON and Lydia A. M. Barton, ward of George French who is surety.

16 March 1816. Garret V. W. RAYMOND and Margaret White, dau. of Henry White who is surety.

13 December 1804. Michael READER and Elizabeth Day, dau. of Sarah Day who consents. Sur. Stephen Winchester.

11 October 1785. William REAT and Ann Minor. Sur. John Wilson.

15 May 1850. William REAVES and Mary Parker. Consent of George W. Parker but no relationship stated. Sur. Arthur Jenkins.

3 January 1816. Hezekiah REEDER and Jemima Suthard. Sur. Timothy Green.

4 July 1844. Philip REES and Sarah Beech, dau. of Ann Williams who consents. Sur. John Toomes.

10 December 1834. Aaron REEVES and Fanny Lewis, dau. of Matilda Lewis and probably Adam Lewis both of whom sign the consent. Sur. George De Baptist.

20 July 1836. Peter REEVES and Jane West. Sur. John James Chew.

17 July 1817. George REVEER and Judah Hughlett. Sur. Jeremiah Parrish. Royston Hughlett makes oath Judah is upwards of 21 but no relationship stated.

28 December 1849. William REVES and Amanda Lee. Sur. William Lee.

6 August 1842. Johnson REYNOLDS and Ann Drinnan./ Sur. Conrad H. Hunt.

15 January 1845. James RICH and Mary Taliaferro. Sur. Walter Williams who makes oath Mary is over 21.

22 December 1818. George B. RICHARDS and Catharine Graham. Sur. William S. Stone who makes oath Catharine is over 21.

26 January 1842. John RICHARDS and Judy Parker. Sur. Edward Parker.

20 February 1811. Robert RICHARDS and Martha H. Jones, dau. of Letitia Jones who consents. Sur. Tinsley Chewning. The following statement dated 20 February 1811, is attached: "I certify that Robert Richards will be twenty-two years of age the 23 day of June next. John Richards."

17 December 1819. John M. RICHARDSON and Virginia Ann Underwood, dau. of John Underwood who is surety.

19 November 1814. Henry RICHARDSON and Maria Backhouse. Sur. Thomas Cary.

31 October 1850. Robert O. RIDGAWAY and Sarah Jane Daingerfield. Sur. James Thornley.

8 February 1838. Lorenso ROBERTS and Mary Ann Donaldson, dau. of Persilla Donaldson. Sur. Samuel McKenzie.

18 November 1834. Samuel ROBERTS and Elizabeth Bryant. Sur. James L. Ege.

26 June 1817. William J. ROBERTS and Martha Lomax. Sur. William A. Gregory.

3 June 1834. Henry R. ROBEY and Clarissa T. Brooks. Sur. William C. C. Abbott.

4 November 1844. Henry R. ROBEY and Susan Frances Brownlow. Sur. John James Chew and John Felt.

24 December 1844. Charles H. ROBINSON and Maria Turner, dau. of Alexander Turner and probably E. Turner who also signs consent. Sur. John James Chew.

23 February 1809. John ROBINSON and Nancy Brown, widow. Sur. Thomas Hall. For proof that Nancy Brown was a widow see the marriage of William H. Lilly and Elizabeth Brown.

18 November 1847. Joseph ROBINSON and Margaret C. Grotz. Sur. John Grotz.

20 December 1821. William P. ROBINSON and Eleanor Pearson, dau. of William Pearson who is surety.

19 November 1840. Jacob F. M. ROCKFELLER and Frances M. Whaling. Sur. Posey Whaling.

9 May 1824. Daniel RODGERS and Anna G. Barefoot. Sur. Thomas Williams.

26 January 1836. Enoch ROLLINS and Lydia Ann Layton. Sur. Robert G. Layton. This name also appears on the bond as Rawlings but is signed quite distinctly Enoch Rollins.

19 May 1835. Henry ROLLINS and Susan Rose, dau. of Margaret Rose of Stafford County. Sur. John L. Knight.

20 March 1834. John J. ROLLOW and Malvira Long, dau. of Joshua Long. Sur. Benjamin Long.

17 January 1825. William ROLLOW and Eliza Ann Shuletice, dau. of John L. Shuletice who is surety.

27 December 1836. George F. ROOTES and Sarah A. White. Sur. George F. Chew.

22 April 1807. Thomas R. ROOTES, Jr. and Anne French, dau. of George French. Sur. William A. Gregory.

2 June 1842. Robert ROSE and Sarah True, dau. of Fanny True. Sur. John Truslow.

8 June 1786. Daniel ROSS and Jean Lindsay. Sur. Tully Whitehurst.

9 November 1819. John ROSS and Mary Brumfield. Sur. D. Herndon.

14 March 1827. George W. ROTHROCK and Louisanna Johnston. Sur. Richard Johnston.

4 November 1850. Rev. John G. ROWE and Margaret A. L. Purcell, dau. of Sarah S. Blackey who consents. Sur. John W. Collins. "Richmond County to wit: This is to authorize the clerk of Spottsylvania Court to issue license for the consumation of the marriage of Mr. John G. Rowe and Margaret A. L. Purcell. October 30, 1850. Sam'l Lyell.

- April 1824. John ROY and Eliza Alexander. Sur. Thomas Seddon.

3 May 1825. William H. ROY and Ann Seddon. Sur. Thomas Seddon.

7 January 1823. Capt. James RUMAGE and Ann Snow, dau. of John Snow who consents and makes oath Ann was 21 on 28 Dec. 1822. Sur. George Revier.

26 September 1834. James RUMMAGE and Lynia Ann White "of Fredericks-burg". Sur. Thomas Crosley who makes oath Lynia Ann is over 21 and has been heretofore married.

14 September 1819. John H. RUNNELS and Eliza B. Dade. Sur. Josiah H. Doe who makes oath Eliza is over 21.

6 April 1824. Benjamin RUST and Frances Davis. Sur. Daniel Davis who makes oath Frances is upward of 21 "and has no father alive".

24 May 1843. James J. RYAN and Susan F. Gordon. Sur. William K. Gordon.

24 October 1818. Archibald RYE and Elizabeth Condiffe. Sur. B. D. Hughlett.

17 March 1845. Benjamin SACREY and Sarah G. Godfrey. Sur. Charles Williams.

7 January 1830. John SAMUEL and Mary Faulkner. Sur. John H. James.

12 October 1815. Philemon SAMUEL and Maria Pitts, ward of George Ellis who is surety.

12 November 1839. Charles H. SANFORD and Julia Ellis Bibb. Sur. Thomas Bibb.

12 September 1839. Captain John SANDS and Pina Donaldson, dau. of Mrs. Prsicilla Donaldson who consents. Sur. Henry Currell.

28 April 1825. Henry SANDY and Charlotte Hill, widow. Sur. David Goldsby.

20 January 1825. Henry SANGER and Elizabeth Whaley. Sur. Edmund Southard.

19 September 1838. Thomas S. SAVAGE and Susan A. Metcalfe. Sur. Richard B. Maury.

18 July 1844. Jacob SCHAUT and Mary Jane Long, dau. of Martha Long of Fredericksburg. Sur. Lewis B. Wood.

2 January 1849. Samuel W. SCHOFIELD and Elizabeth Rennolds, dau. of Elizabeth Rennolds who consents. Her father is dead. Sur. Guilford Edrington.

21 July 1817. Thomas T. SCHOFIELD and Catherine Coleman. Sur. Charles S. Johnston who makes oath Catherine is 21.

30 May 1837. John F. SCHRICKEL and Mary M. King. Sur. Isaac M. King.

1 October 1838. Francis W. SCOTT and Ann M. Minor. Sur. William A. Jackson.

5 March 1834. James M. SCOTT and Mary S. Lefene. Sur. William H. Luckett. Charles W. Castleman, guardian of Mary S. Lefene, of Frederick County, Virginia, gives his consent to the marriage.

18 October 1838. Robert E. SCOTT and Ann Morson. Sur. Arthur A. Morson.

5 December 1815. Thomas C. Scott and Mary L. Seddon. Sur. George F. Vowles. Thomas Seddon of Falmouth, Virginia, guardian of Mary writes his consent.

25 April 1848. John SEDDON and Mary A. Little. Sur. John S. Wellford.

1 June 1836. Joseph W. SENER and Mary Ann Raines. Sur. Francis Mills.

5 May 1815. John SEXSMITH and Mildred Summers. Sur. Joseph Walker.

23 September 1834. William B. B. SEWARD and Mary McWilliams, dau. of Clara McWilliams who consents. Sur. William B. Davis.

11 January 1820. James SEWELL and Eliza Sexsmith. Sur. George Sexsmith who makes oath Eliza is 21.

11 August 1835. Abraham SHADLAR and Elizabeth Kennedy, dau. of Mary Kennedy who consents. Sur. Andrew Kennedy and Mary Kennedy.

29 July 1785. Dennis SHAY and Mary Feomer (this surname is very indistinct). Sur. William Murray.

7 December 1841. John SHEETS and Virginia L. Quisenberry. Sur. William Quisenberry.

8 October 1850. John SHELTON and Nancy Bates. Sur. George L. Bowling.

10 January 1833. Wallace SHELTON and Susan Ann Briscoe, dau. of Many (or Mary) Briscoe. Sur. Robert White.

28 May 1808. John M. SHEPHERD and Judith Benson, dau. of J. Benson who consents. Sur. Peter R. Johnson.

5 September 1826. William U. SHORT and Mrs. Fanny Warfield. Sur. Philip August.

13 September 1804. John L. SHOULTRICE and Sally Davis, dau. of William Davis who consents. Sur. Richard Peacock. Bond signed in German, John Leonard Shultice.

11 April 1805. Francis SHOVELER and Charlotte Porch, dau. of Easham Porch who consents. Sur. Samuel Davis. Bond signed in German.

11 February 1837. J. L. SIBLEY and Mary Hewlitt. Sur. Samuel McKinsey.

9 June 1823. James SILLS and Mildred Puzey, dau. of Alden Puzey who is surety.

8 July 1813. Josiah SIMPSON and Ann H. Stanard. Sur. John Taliaferro.

11 April 1831. Howard SIMS and Catherine Henry. Sur. Roland Wood.

21 September 1820. Nimrod SIMS and Nancy Bowling. Sur. Lewis Courtney.

28 November 1803. Samuel SKINKER and Margaret Julian. Sur. Charles Julian. Samuel Skinker son of William Skinker.

19 October 1820. William SKINKER and Sarah Nickens. Sur. William
(continued)

48

Bedford. Bond states "Both free person of colour". Hugh Atchinson
of Stafford County, legal guardian of William Skinker gives his
consent to marriage.

5 April 1830. Humberston SKIPWITH and Lelia Robertson. Sur. Dr.
Edward H. Barton.

11 November 1817. Samuel SLAUGHTER and Virginia Stanard. Married
by the Rev. Edward C. McGuire, Rector of St. George's Parish.
Ministers' Returns.

29 January 1826. Noah SMALL and Nancy Hughlett. Sur. John Taylor.

25 February 1829. Austin SMITH and Mary Miller Buck. Sur. Anthony
Buck.

13 December 1832. Benjamin H. SMITH and Fenton Brooke. Sur. John
James Chew. Ministers' Returns say Grace Fenton Brooke.

13 November 1811. Charles H. SMITH and Evelina Stone, dau. of
William S. Stone who consents. Sur. Dabney Herndon.

6 August 1807. David SMITH and Eleanor Frazer, dau. of Bridget
Frazer who consents saying Eleanor's father is dead. Sur. George
Welch.

14 February 1825. George A. SMITH and Ophelia A. Williams. Sur.
Isaac H. Williams.

25 June 1833. Henry SMITH and Virginia E. Taylor. Sur. Edward H.
Carmichael.

3 March 1819. John SMITH and Alice Wolfe, dau. of Grace Fenton
Wolfe who is surety.

29 June 1826. John H. SMITH and Margaret Buck, dau. of Anthony
Buck who is surety.

5 December 1812. Robert SMITH and Hannah Walker. Sur. Peter Cotton.
Hannah Walker states she is a widow, over 21, a resident of Fredericksburg. She desires the clerk to issue license for her intermarriage
with Robert Smith of Maryland.

28 February 1836. Robert SMITH and Margaret Pritchard. Sur. John
Pritchard.

19 June 1845. Robert SMITH and Ann Middleton. Sur. George F. Chew.

27 October 1806. Samuel SMITH and Eleanor Mark. Married by the Rev.
S. B. Wilson. Ministers' Returns.

31 July 1843. Dr. William M. SMITH and Harriet C. Wishart, ward of John Metcalf who consents. Sur. John L. Marye.

28 May 1839. William P. SMITH and Marion M. Seddon, dau. of Susan P. Seddon who consents, stating Marion is under 21 years old. Sur. James A. Seddon.

16 October 1813. Esme SMOCK and Sarah H. Richards. Sur. William Smock.

16 May 1818. William SMOCK and Sarah White, widow. Sur. William Jackson.

4 October 1810. Thomas SNOW and Elizabeth Morgan who makes oath she is over 21 and that both her parents are dead; she has no legal guardian. Sur. John Snow, father of said Thomas Snow.

27 February 1821. William K. SNYDER and Mary Pope, widow. Sur. Joshua Myers.

5 January 1849. John SOLAN and Martha Ann King. Sur. William King.

9 October 1827. Dr. Walter SOMMERVILLE and Mary H. Briggs, dau. of D. Briggs who gives his consent. Sur. Henry Sommerville.

30 September 1817. Carter SORRELL and Elizabeth Penny. Sur. Thomas Daniel.

9 November 1831. James P. SORRELL and Emily Mardes, dau. of William Mardes who consents. Sur. William H. Bradshaw and Alexander Sorrell.

14 October 1840. James M. SOUTHARD and Lucy Ann Frazer. Sur. James Frazer.

29 May 1832. James T. SOUTTER and Agnes G. Knox, dau. of Mrs. Sarah C. Knox who makes oath Agnes is under 21 and that her father William A. Knox is dead. She gives her consent. Sur. Philip Alexander. James T. Soutter of Norfolk, Virginia.

29 October 1846. Martin SPICER and Elminey Staiars. Sur. R. Staiars.

5 September 1839. James W. SPILLMAN and Martha L. Baggett, dau. of Judith C. Baggatt who writes her consent. Sur. Charles A. Shepherd.

9 January 1832. Thomas W. SPILMAN and Ann Cox, dau. of George Cox who consents. Sur. Albert G. Lucas.

7 March 1787. John STAMPER and Susannah B. Young. Sur. Luke Mullancaure.

50

23 August 1815. John STANARD and Caroline Matilda Chew. Sur. Robert S. Chew.

5 June 1803. William STEPHENS and Sally Jordan, dau. of Joseph Jordan who consents and is surety. Wit. Joseph Jordan, Jr. and Jeremiah Jordan.

5 July 1837. John STERLING and Catharine Ashby, dau. of Margaret R. Ashby who consents. Sur. George Ayler.

1 August 1840. Richard STERLING and Marian Howison. Sur. Samuel Howison.

19 September 1818. Hugh STEVENS and Mary Doggett. Sur. Lemuel Doggett who makes oath that both parties are over 21, also, that both parents of Mary Doggett are deceased.

31 January 1849. James STEVENS and Ann Allen. Sur. Edward Finney.

26 May 1847. Monroe STEVENS and Elizabeth Robinson. Sur. James Proctor. William King makes oath Elizabeth is over 21; no relationship between the two parties is stated.

24 December 1814. Reuben STEVENS and Mary M. Moore. Sur. Timothy Green.

8 March 1809. Carter L. STEVENSON and Jane Whitter Herndon, dau. of William Herndon who consents. Sur. Robert S. Chew.

8 February 1818. Richard Lewis STEVENSON and Amanda M. Herndon. Married by the Rev. Edward C. McGuire, Rector of St. George's Parish. Ministers' Returns.

22 April 1828. James M. STHRESHLEY and Mary P. B. Fitzhugh, dau. of Frances T. Fitzhugh who gives her consent. Sur. William H. Buckner.

24 January 1824. Armistead STOKERS and Sally McTyre. Sur. Robert Hudgin. The groom's name is also spelled Stocas. The bride's name is also spelled Mackteentiar.

2 September 1846. Edward STONE and Mary Crossley. Sur. J. W. Jenkins.

2 October 1812. George STREBECK and Susannah Sidney Graham. Sur. John Scott.

1 June 1820. John STRICKLER and Martha Crawford, widow. Sur. James Long.

26 April 1832. William STROTHER and Evilina West. Sur. James West, Jr.

29 February 1820. Charles B. STUART and Maria Thornton. Sur, John S. Thornton.

16 April 1806. James STUART and Elizabeth Maxwell. Sur. James L. Drinan.

31 October 1838. Abraham SULLIVAN and Sarah Ann Wilkins. Sur. Jones Wilkins.

20 March 1833. Spencer S. SULLIVAN and Mary W. Williams, dau. of Elizabeth Williams who gives her consent. Sur. William Cox.

25 February 1835. James SUTHARD, Jr. and Mary J. Perry. Sur. James Suthard, Sr. Hiram Perry makes oath Mary is over 21.

12 September 1850. Christian H. SWATS and Sarah A. True. Sur. Dolphin True.

28 January 1806. Morgan SWEENEY and Sarah Waddell, dau.-in-law (step-dau), David Almond who is surety.

27 June 1818. Morgan SWEENEY and Pamelia Phillips. Sur. Henry T. Phillips.

29 May 1846. Robert S. SWORDE and Marie Louise Stanard. Sur. John B. Stanard.

25 October 1843. Charles A. TACKETT and Frances Ford. Sur. James W. Ford.

8 September 1845. John E. TACKETT and Sophia Ford. Sur. James W. Ford.

22 October 1845. Claiborne TALIAFERRO and Virginia De Baptist, probably dau. of Edward De Baptist. Sur. Walter Williams.

20 October 1832. Francis W. TALIAFERRO and Catharine Ware. Sur. John James Chew.

18 November 1834. James TALIAFERRO and Mahallen Ann Walker. Sur. James Wilkins. This bride's name also spelled Mahaley.

6 September 1809. Lewis W. TALIAFERRO and Polly Stanard. Sur. Walker R. Carter.

10 November 1825. Peachy R. TALIAFERRO and Sarah F. Adams. Sur. Thomas B. Adams. Peachy son of Richard H. Taliaferro.

27 October 1825. Warner T. TALIAFERRO and Leah Seddon, dau. of Thomas Seddon who is surety.

17 May 1842. William TALIAFERRO and Maria West. Sur. Edward De Baptist.

15 October 1836. William TARR and Clementine Garner. Sur. Jesse Pullin.

1 August 1849. Albert T. TAYLOR and Jane Alice Cridlin, dau. of William Cridlin who gives his consent. Sur. Henry J. Reamy.

6 March 1830. Evan TAYLOR and Ann W. Batley, widow. Sur. Charles Chrismond. Thomas Chrismond makes oath Ann W. Batley is over 21 and a widow.

25 October 1843. Henry TAYLOR and Margaret Jones, dau. of Isaac Jones who is surety.

1 January 1824. Ivan TAYLOR and Alice Thompson. Sur. Lemuel Thompson.

7 February 1839. James A. TAYLOR and Mildred Wren. Sur. William M. Cannon.

6 August 1817. Capt. John TAYLOR and Mildred Hughlett. Sur. Archibald Rye. Beder Hughlett makes oath his sister Milly Hughlett is of age.

20 November 1823. John TAYLOR and Lucy Brooke. Sur. Thomas Cary.

12 September 1834. Dr. John TAYLOR and Marion Gordon, dau. of Samuel Gordon. Sur. William E. Voss.

26 February 1850. Joshua T. TAYLOR and Maria Louisa Long. Sur. J. H. Beck.

6 November 1835. Thornton TAYLOR and Eleanor Baxter, dau. of Thornton Baxter who writes his consent. Sur. Ransom Baxter. Name also written Ellen Baxter on the bond.

13 December 1820. Capt. Thomas TAYLOR, Sr. and Fanny Reveer. Sur. George Reveer.

17 May 1817. Thomas TAYLOR, Jr. and Margaret Pearson whose sister Catherine August makes oath she is over 21. Sur. Thomas Snow. Thomas Taylor, Sr. makes oath his son Thomas was born 19 May 1793. Wit. John Snow. The signature on that statement is identical with the above marriage of Capt. Thomas Taylor, Sr. If Thomas, Jr. was born 1793 he was son of Capt. Thomas Taylor's first marriage.

21 December 1833. William TAYLOR and Mary Ann Allison, a servant girl belonging to Jane Walker who gives her consent to marriage. Sur. Benjamin Clarke.

16 October 1834. William TAYLOR and Lucy Lewis Thom. Sur. Reuben T. Thom. Original bond says William Taylor is "of pt. Corper"; What does this mean?

18 June 1845. Joseph P. TERRELL and Maria H. W. Noel. Sur. James Cooke.

26 September 1832. Oliver TERRILL and Susan Elizabeth Proctor. Sur. Thomas Proctor.

8 January 1824. Thomas TERRIER and Elizabeth Batchelder, ward of Daniel G. Reid who is surety. John Terrier makes oath Thomas Terrier is over 21.

19 December 1842. Barnabus B. THAYER and Sarah W. Cowne, dau. of Balinger Cowne. Sur. Albert Hooton.

13 November 1835. James THOMAS and Jane Pedler. Sur. George W. Parrott.

26 September 1842. William H. THOMAS and Ann E. Riley. Sur. Lewis Burke.

17 March 1830. James E. THOMSON and Caroline M. Fitzhugh, dau. of Frances T. Fitzhugh. Sur. Dr. Jefferson Minor.

30 October 1815. Joseph D. THOMSON and Catharine Garder or Gardner. Sur. John Sexsmith.

16 December 1830. Robert D. THORBURN and Helen M. Howison. Sur. Samuel Howison.

5 January 1826. James D. THORBURN and Ann M. Howison, dau. of Samuel Howison who is surety.

29 December 1810. Anthony R. THORNTON and Mildred B. Walker, ward of William James who gives his consent to marriage. Sur. Benjamin G. Thornton.

30 November 1815. John S. THORNTON and Susan H. Gordon. Married by the Rev. Edward C. McGuire, Rector of St. George's Parish. Ministers' Returns.

17 September 1838. Thomas S. THORNTON and Isabella Layton. Sur. Enoch Rollins.

15 February 1844. William THORNTON and Ann Pritchard. Sur. John Pritchard.

11 October 1838. Daniel TIBBS and Jane Belfour. Sur. W.P. Conway. Duff Green makes oath Jane Belfour is a free girl of colour and is over 21.

8 February 1836. John TIMBERLAKE and Jane J. Peyton. Sur. John Peyton.

29 June 1805. John W. TIMBERLAKE and Mary Garetson. Sur. Isaac Garretson.

20 September 1815. Joseph TIMBERLAKE and Elizabeth Benson, dau. of John Benson, deceased. Sur. Alexander Walker.

24 May 1843. James B. TIMBERLAKE and Sarah A. Walker. Sur. John G. Parish.

18 April 1837. John C. TOLSON and Jane Catherine Mills, dau. of James Mills who is surety.

14 June 1836. Joseph T. TOMPKINS and Jane Ford, dau. of Patsy Ford who writes her consent. Wit. Margaret Freeman. Sur. John Ferney-hough.

7 April 1835. Robert R. TOMPKINS and Elizabeth T. Fitzgerald, dau. of James H. Fitzgerald. Sur. Henry R. Robey.

21 October 1829. William TRAINER and Catharine Bryant, dau. of Rosannah Bryant who makes cath Catharine is 21. Sur. Jesse White and Lewis Burke.

25 April 1850. Henry TRIGGER and Ellen Lawson, sister of Catlett Lawson who makes oath Ellen is 21. Sur. Ryland Mullen.

19 May 1813. John R. TRIPLETT and Louisa R. Stone. Sur. Charles H. Smith.

17 January 1844. William S. TRIPLETT and Ann O. Jenifer. Sur. William S. Barton.

26 May 1847. Edward E. TRUE and Lucinda Lawson. Sur. John Fitchett.

5 July 1837. William TRUE and Susannah Jane Curtis. Sur. John James Chew.

28 September 1846. Walter A. TRUE and Ann E. Mullen. Sur. Ryland Mullen.

2 May 1842. John TRUSLOW and Martha True, dau. of Fanny True who writes her consent. Sur. Daniel B. Rodgers.

27 October 1847. Robert TRUSLOW and Orphy L. Fugett. Sur. William True.

4 July 1787. Francis TUPMAN and Sarah Lucas. Sur. Fielding Lucas.

13 January 1825. Thomas G. TUPMAN and Louisianna Wardell. Sur. William Smock.

21 September 1826. William B. TUPMAN and Ann Slater, ward of Robert Dickey who is surety.

3 January 1828. George TURNER and Philadelphia C. Frazer. Sur. John Chew.

9 December 1845. James A. TURNER and Susan Q. Johnson. Sur. Albert Hooten.

27 February 1816. Thomas TUTT and Margaret W. Garnett, daughter-in-law (step-dau.?) of Richard J. Tutt who is surety.

10 October 1839. William W. TYLER and Fanny A. Stevenson. Sur. John M. Speed.

1 November 1837. John UNDERWOOD and Jane Hill. Sur. John P. Hill.

2 June 1785. Charles URQUHART and Finella Duncanson, dau. of James Duncanson. Sur. Armistead Long.

24 December 1850. William VAUGHAN and Eliza Jane Norton. Sur. Charles Layton.

27 September 1843. James VESSELS and Elizabeth Parker. Sur. Edward Parker.

29 January 1846. James Alexander WADDELL and Cornelia Lomax. Sur. P. Thornton Lomax.

19 February 1821. James A. WADDLE and Louisa Chewning. Sur. John Chewning.

18 April 1827. William WAGON and Elizabeth Lewis. Sur. Lewis Burke. This name may be Wogon, Wogan or Wagan.

26 February 1826. Harris WALKER and Margaret Caldwell. Sur. John S. Caldwell.

4 January 1849. James WALKER and Jane L. Lowery. Sur. William T. Lowery.

24 March 1847. John B. WALKER and Permelia P. Paine. Sur. M.A. Blackman makes oath that Permelia P. Paine has resided with his family for several weeks past and that she is a native of New York and came to Fredericksburg with the intention of teaching school and with no intention of returning to New York.

12 March 1829. James N. WALKER and Mary E. Sorrelle. Sur. James Peyton.

15 October 1845. William G. WALKER and Mary Ellen Taylor. Sur. Adelph Richards.

27 September 1828. Dr. John H. WALLACE and Mary N. Gordon, dau. of Samuel Gordon who writes his consent. Sur. John James Chew.

6 February 1840. Richard WALLACE and Mary Louisa Ames, dau. of Nany Ames who consents. Sur. John S. Caldwell.

8 October 1845. Gustavus B. WALLACE and Elizabeth Macfarlane. Sur. John Minor.

3 October 1820. George WALLER and Harriet Alexander, dau. of Lewis Alexander who is surety.

12 May 1825. Robert Page WALLER and Julia W. Mercer. Sur. Hugh Mercer.

19 December 1822. William WALLER and Ann A. Lucas, dau. of Zachariah Lucas who gives his consent. Sur. Harrison T. Lucas.

- - - . WALLINGFORD - see Wolingford.

1 April 1807. Thomas WARE and Catherine Reat. Sur. Reubin T. Thom.

11 February 1804. Alexander WARFIELD and Fanny Sacrae, dau. of Thomas Sacrae. Sur. Robert McKildoe. This bond is signed Warfield but in the body of the bond it is written Waughfield.

29 December 1825. Thomas WARING and Phiana H. Mathews. Sur. John T. Owilbar.

15 December 1819. William WARREN and Ann Bowen. Sur. Alexander Walker.

24 July 1833. Alexander WATERS and Mary Ninnes. Sur. James W. Newby.

13 December 1821. Laurence WAUGH and Sidney Smith Roddy, ward of Yeamans Smith who consent and is surety.

25 October 1830. Lawrence WAUGH and Lavinia W. Wigglesworth. Sur. Robert C. Bruce.

15 February 1837. Charles B. WAYT and Eliza M. Whitehurst. Sur. James E. Dishman.

7 January 1837. James WAYT and Sarah C. Rose. Sur. Charles B. Wayt.

30 May 1831. George WAYTE and Mary Cuppenhaven. Sur. Benjamin R. Hillyard.

27 March 1839. Joseph WEBB and Clara Evans. Sur. James McDowner.

22 December 1832. Thomas WEEMS and Ellen Boores. Sur. Alexander K. Phillips.

7 June 1837. George WEIR and Ellen Jones. Sur. Henry Stevens.

4 February 1824. Beverley R. WELLFORD and Mary Alexander. Sur. Philip Alexander.

14 March 1820. John S. WELLFORD and Jane Henderson. Sur. Hugh Nelson.

24 May 1839. Robert WELLFORD and Fanny L. Stevenson. Robert Wellford is ward of Beverley R. Wellford who consents and is surety. Fanny L. Stevenson is ward of John Metcalfe who gives his consent.

20 April 1839. William T. WELLS and Sarah Pullen. Sur. Jesse Pullen.

5 February 1845. Baylor WEST and Mary Ellen Chapman, dau. of Page Thornton who consents. Sur. James West.

11 July 1812. Isaac WEST and Fanny Stribling. Sur. William Stribling.

23 October 1833. James WEST and Patsy Richardson. Sur. John James Chew.

23 November 1842. Thomas Bowling WEST and Louisa Mildred Phillips. Sur. Alexander K. Phillips.

4 February 1786. Thomas WESTON and Ann Moore. Sur. Christopher Donaly.

2 December 1850. Alexander L. WHALING and Ann V. Haydon. Sur. John Haydon, Jr.

18 August 1846. John Addison WHEELER and Virginia Long. Sur. Jacob Schaut.

9 November 1837. William WHEELER and Mary M. Godfrey. Sur. George Alor.

10 April 1819. Francis C. WHISTON and Eliza F. Garnett, ward of David Briggs who gives his consent. Sur. John Peck.

11 December 1844. Alfred WHITE and Charlotte Corr. Sur. William Mann.

27 January 1830. Ambrose L. WHITE and Frances Ragan. Sur. John Ferneyhough.

16 September 1803. Henry WHITE and Elizabeth Peacock. Sur. William Pearson.

14 July 1828. Robert WHITE and Margaret Fortune. Sur. Thomas Proctor.

20 January 1831. Henry M. WHITEHURST and Eliza M. Towles. Sur. John L. Whaley.

29 July 1812. John WHITING and Elizabeth Scags, dau. of Catharine Boores who gives her consent. Sur. Thornton Keys.

17 January 1831. John M. WHITTEMORE and Martha E. Lucas. Sur. Albert G. Lucas.

26 October 1818. Capt. Claiborne WIGLESWORTH and Lavinia Ward Farish, ward of Yeamans Smith who is surety.

28 December 1846. James Henry WILKERSON and Catharine L. Chapman. Sur. Willis Washington.

24 November 1831. Bland WILLIAMS and Susan Bell. Sur. Marshall Johnson.

23 February 1843. Henry A. WILLIAMS and Mary Elder. Sur. John D. Elder.

12 December 1815. James WILLIAMS and Margaret Smith. Sur. William P. Goodwin.

31 August 1837. James L. WILLIAMS and Ann Beach. Sur. William H. Fulcher, Jr.

3 February 1810. Capt. John WILLIAMS and Elizabeth Reeves, dau. of Mary Reeves who gives her consent and makes oath Elizabeth is "of lawful age". Sur. Adam Donaldson.

24 April 1819. Joseph WILLIAMS and Anne Smallwood. Sur. Gilson Arrington.

21 December 1820. Richard WILLIAMS and Elizabeth Smock, dau. of William Smock who gives his consent very quaintly as follows: "Sir: You will please grant a lisens of marriage to Mr. Richard Williams & my daughter Elizabeth Smock. Given under my hand. Wm. Smock, Frdckg. Dec. 21st 1820. Robert S. Chew, Clerk of the Court". Robert S. Chew, clerk, wrote as follows: "No witness, but I know the old man's signature and furthermore both parties are old enough to do the thing without his leave". Sur. James Harrison.

24 November 1829. Robert M. WILLIAMS and Melinda Ingram. Sur. Lamuel J. Thompson.

20 May 1850. Tandy WILLIAMS and Elizabeth Jane Parker. Sur. Arthur Jenkins. Robert Parker makes oath Elizabeth is over 21; no relationship indicated.

8 January 1831. Thomas WILLIAMS and Hannah Tarkelson. Sur. Peter P. Cox. Bride's name also spelled Tarkleson in bond.

7 October 1837. Walter WILLIAMS and Catharine G. Edmondson. Sur. John W. Edmondson.

17 December 1817. William T. WILLIAMS and Ann Newby, dau. of J. Newby who gives his consent. Sur. Thomas Ware.

20 October 1841. Washington WILLIE and May Crump. Sur. John Crump.

8 November 1838. Benjamin N. WILLIS and Charlotte U. Briggs. Sur. George Aler.

16 June 1810. Lewis WILLIS and Elizabeth Brumfield. Sur. Carter L. Stevenson.

9 June 1846. William H. WILLIS and Eliza White. Sur. William White, Jr.

22 November 1832. David WILSON and Lucy U. Batchelder. Sur. Thomas Terrier.

3 March 1804. Reubin WILSON and Eliza A. Dillard, dau. of Francis Dillard who gives consent. Sur. George M. Wilson.

19 March 1845. William WIRT and Betty S. Payne. Sur. Lawrence W. Berry.

8 March 1841. Walter WITHERS and Margaret M. Baggott. Sur. John J. Berry.

24 July 1843. Thomas R. WOLFE and Maria B. Temple. Sur. William A. Jackson.

31 August 1842. John W. WOLINGFORD and Jane Williams. Sur. Henry A. Williams. This name also appears as Wallingford on the bond.

27 June 1805. John WOOD and Nancy Johnson, dau. of Benjamin Johnson who writes consent. Wit. Susanna Johnson. Sur. David Ollins.

17 April 1816. Silas WOOD and Julia Anne Brock. Sur. R. S. Chew.

24 June 1840. Singleton WOOD and Eliza Jane Mackay, dau. of Maria L. Mackay who gives her consent. Sur. James McGuire.

8 August 1831. Aaron WOODS and Ann Grigsby Grinnan. Sur. Henry William Grinnan.

23 December 1841. Freeborn WOODSON and Eliza Garner. Sur. James Mondowney.

17 September 1833. John T. WORMELEY and Virginia F. Holt. Sur. John W. West.

2 December 1807. Warner L. WORMLEY and Maria Hall. Sur. David Henderson, Jr.

14 February 1838. Albert W. WRENN and Catharine E. Benson. Sur. Landon J. Huffman.

20 September 1842. Lewis WREN and Eliza Pilcher. Sur. John L. Marye. This name is written Wrenn in the bond but signed Wren.

- May 1815. Thomas WREN and Malinda Mills. Married by the Rev. William James. Ministers' Returns.

16 April 1828. James C. WRIGHT and Lucy Ann Burden, dau. of Elizabeth Burden who gives her consent. Sur. Archibald Burden.

13 October 1842. James C. WRIGHT and Jane Southard. Sur. John J. Rollow. The signature on this bond is identical with the one above signifying they must be the same man.

27 October 1818. John S. WRIGHT and Charlotte Pendleton, dau. of Robert Pendleton who is surety.

16 April 1828. Stapleton C. WRIGHT and Jane P. Sorrell. Sur. Alexander Sorrell.

19 May 1807. Thomas WRIGHT and Ann ("Nancy") Norwood. Sur. James Slater. The name also appears as Right in the bond, but, since it is filed in the W's, this seems to be the logical place for it.

28 May 1850. George W. WROTEN and Sarah W. Rollow. Sur. Henry D. Genther. This name appears in bond as Wroughton but is signed Wroten.

- . WROUGHTON - see Wroten

23 July 1827. Capt. Stewart WROUGHTON and Mildred Layton, dau. of John Layton who gives consent to the marriage. Sur. Horace Clark.

13 January 1845. Stewart WROUGHTON and Sarah King. Sur. William F. King.

23 May 1833. John B. YATES and Elizabeth Murray, dau. of Elizabeth Murray who gives her consent. Sur. George H. Whitercarver. John B. Yates son of George Yates of Rappahannock County, who writes his consent to the marriage.

16 December 1824. John W. YEATMAN and Mary Ann Boyle, ward of Perry Kelley who is surety. This note accompanies the bond: "Mr. John Yeatman the Bearer of this, served his apprenticeship with me and was twenty-one years of age on ye 17th day of Feby last say 1824. W. Smock."

12 October 1812. Thomas YERBY and Elizabeth Callett. Sur. John Brown. The Bride's name may be Catlett. This note accompanies the bond: "This is to certify that Mrs. Brent the mother of Thomas Yerby affirms he was born the 12th of October 1791. Cyrus Coppedge, Guardian to Thos. Yerby".

6 August 1818. Thomas YEARBY and Harriot Pratt. Married by the Rev. Edward C. McGuire, Rector of St. George's Parish. Ministers' Returns.

17 July 1845. Henry YOUNG and Elizabeth Burnett. Sur. William De Baptist.

20 October 1825. William YOUNG and Melinda Ferrell. Sur. Leeson Ferrell.

Saint George's Cemetery

Saint George Parish was laid out by Act of the Virginia General Assembly in 1720. In 1727 Fredericksburg was founded, and it is thought interments began at Saint George's Cemetery about this time.

In 1892 the cemetery was greatly neglected, and the LADIES CEMETERY GUILD OF ST. GEORGE'S CHURCH undertook to clean it up and place it in good condition. At this time several of the gravestones were repaired and other improvements made. This guild was lead by Miss Nannie S. Goodwin, President; Miss Lizzie Rennolds, Treasurer; and Miss Alice R. Gordon, Secretary – all now deceased.

Under their direction the Rev. W. M. Clark published "St. George's Cemetery: An Historical Sketch" in which he gives a brief history of the parish and a list of the tombstones then in the cemetery with the date (year only) the party died and their age at that time. In this list he also includes names "of all buried in St. George's Church-yard as far as can be ascertained".

The following inscriptions were copied in 1940 by me and carefully checked. Whenever there is doubt as to a letter or figure, same will be noted. No doubt if I had had the pleasure of copying these stone in 1890, we would have had a few more inscriptions than we now are able to present. We also learn that numerous upright stone were broken during the bombardment of Fredericksburg during the War Between the States.

Some of the stones are fastly disintegrating and crumbleing away, while others are exceptionally well preserved.

There are undoubtedly scores of persons buried here of which we have no record, and many are buried where we now see side walks, streets, and buildings. On 27 March 1802 the grand jury of Fredericksburg presented "as a nuisance the numerous obstructions in the streets, particularly in St. George Street lot, burying the dead in George and Princess Ann Streets"...

In making this copy of the tombstones in Saint George's Churchyard I had but one purpose in mind, viz: preserving these inscriptions for posterity well knowing that ere long many will not be decipherable.

George H. S. King

Fredericksburg
January, 1942

ALLEN, MARY

"In Memory of
MARY
daughter of
James and Elizabeth Allen
Born July 25th 1801
Died August 4th 1836
Blessed are the dead which die in the Lord
from henceforth Yes Saith the Spirit, that
they may rest from their labours and their
works do follow them."

ALLEN, WILLIAM & ANN TURNER

"William Allen
Died 1866

And his wife
Ann Turner Allen
Died 1875"

ASHBY, WILLIAM M.

"William M. Ashby
son of Vivion & Margaret
Died
May 31st 1815
Aged 1 Mo: & 15 da:"

BAGGOTT, JAMES

"In MEMORY OF
JAMES BAGGOTT
a native of this town
Born 5th of June
1764
Died 1st of March
1825
Much lamented by those
who knew him best."

BAILEY, CHESTER

"SACRED TO THE MEMORY OF
CHESTER BAILEY
who was born in
Wallingford in Connecticut
August 12, 1769
and departed this life
March 22, 1841
in 72 year of his age."

66

BALL, R. W.
>"R. W. Ball, only child of
Major Cyrus and Fedelia Ball of
of Lancaster County, Virginia.
Died February 17, 1826
Aged 17 years
& 5 months."

BARTON, EDWARD SETH
>"Sacred in Memory of
Edward Seth Barton
second son of
Thomas R. & Susan C. Barton
who departed this life
on the 6th of December 1823
aged 2 years and 21 days. "

BARTON, SETH
>"Here lies an affectionate parent
and sincere friend
Seth Barton
Was born near Warren, Rhode Island,
July 29 A.D. 1755, and died at his
seat near Fredericksburgh, December
29 A.D. 1813, Aged 58 years and 5 months."

BENSON, MRS. ELEANOR
>"To the Memory of
Mrs. Eleanor Benson
who departed this
life the 22nd of May 1799
Aged 38 years."

BERRY, JOHN SCOTT
>"Entered into this life
Dec. 7, 1841
John Scott Berry
son of
Lawrence W* & Ann Scott Berry
Entered into life eternal
Sunday morning
Sept.26, 1920.
A sinner saved by grace."

*M - This is distinctly M, but it clearly should be Lawrence W.
Berry whose tomb is adjacent and who the said Lawrence (1841-1920)
was definitely the son of.

BERRY, LAWRENCE W. & ANNE M.
              "In Memory of Lawrence W. Berry
              Born on the 13th day of Dec. 1792
              and died on 3d February 1846.
              And near are the remains of two
              infant children John in his third
              year and Catherine in her fifth year.
                      On the left
                      Anne M. Berry
                       the wife & Mother
                      Born June 16, 1801
                      Died Sept. 28, 1872."

BEVERLY, CARTER
                  "Carter Beverly
                  Born at Blandfield
                  Essex county, Va.
                  15 of Aug:1774
                  Died F** 10 1844."

    (**) The dates are very indistinct and especially
    what we suspose to be "Feb.10".

BLACKEY, MRS. MARIA ANN
                  "Sacred to the
                  Memory of
                  Maria Ann
                  wife of
              James G. Blakey
          who departed this life
              Aug. 14, 1845
      Aged 42 years & 2 months."

BOUGHTON, BENJAMIN
                  "Benj: Boughton
                  aged 65
                  Died 3d June 1842"

CARTER, ELIZABETH
                  "In Memory of
                  Elizabeth
              daughter of
          Edwain & Elizabeth E. P. Carter
              who died April 29th 1833
      Aged 2 Months & 20 days. "

CARTER, ELIZABETH EDMONDSON
                  "In Memory of
              Elizabeth Edmondson
          daughter of Edwin & Elizabeth E.P. Carter
          who died Sept. 13th 1840. Aged 16 Months
                  & 2 days."

CARLIN, MRS. MARY JANE (CHEWNING)
                    "Grandma
                Mrs. M. J. Carlin
                entered into rest
                April 4, 1885
                in the 76th year of her age."

The lone tombstone is within the only iron fence
enclosure in St. George's Churchyard on the gate of
which is "J.M. Whittemore". The Historical Sketch of
1892 lists her name as Mrs. Mary Jane (Chewning) Carlin.

CHEW, MRS. ANN
                    "Sacred to
                The Memory of
                    Ann Chew
                Relict of
                Capt. John Chew
            who died Oct. 7th 1821
        in the 67th year of her age.

Few Females were more eminantly distinguished for
correctness of deportment and ✻✻✻✻✻✻✻✻✻✻✻✻✻✻✻✻
practice of all the christian virtues. ✻✻✻✻✻✻
was Conjugal as a widow, exemplary as a M✻✻✻✻✻✻✻
fond and affectionate as a neighbour, charitable
and kind as a friend, steady and sincere.

Into thy hands I commend my spirit
For thou has redeemed me,
O Lord God of Truth."

✻✻✻✻✻✻/ One corner of stone is broken.

CHEW, MISS LUCY
                    "In Memory of
                Miss Lucy Chew
                daughter of the late
                John Chew, Esquire, of
                    Spotsylvania.
        Died on the 5th of October 1815.
        Go spotless honor and unsullied truth
        Go smiling innocence
        Go soft humanity that blessed the poor
        Go saint and patience
        Go modesty and never wore a frown
        To virtue and receive the Heavenly Crown."

COAKLEY, CATHERINE
                    "In Memory of
                    Catherine
                the daughter of
                John and Mary Coakley
            who departed this life August 24, 1811
        Aged 8 years and 2 months."

COAKLEY, MRS. ELIZABETH
"Sacred to
the Memory of
Elizabeth Coakley
Relict of
John Coakley
Died March 11, 1890."
The Historical Sketch of 1892 gives her age as 80.

COAKLEY, JOHN
"Entered into Rest
John Coakley
Born Feb. 14, 1805
Died July 2, 1874"

COAKLEY, JOHN
"In Memory of
John, son of
John and Mary Coakley
who departed this life
July 21st, 1794
Aged 3 Years and 1 Month"

COAKLEY, MARY
"Sacred
to the memory of
Mary, Daughter of
John & Elizabeth Coakley
who departed this life
June the 7, 1867 in the
28 year of her age."

C., E.
"1814
E.C."
This small stone so marked is immediately adjacent to
the handsome tomb of Judge John Coalter.

COALTER, JUDGE JOHN
"This stone is erected in Memory of
John Coalter
of Chatham
Of humble origin, he rose to eminence less by the display
of uncommon talents than by moral worth. By an integrity
that none ever questioned. A fidelity that evaded no duty.
A firmness that defied a like temptation and danger. And a
sincerity simplicity and kindness of nature that won the hearts
of all who approached him. The records of his country testify
the honourable posts which he filled. Of his private virtues
all who knew him can speak.
(next page)

- continued
But the depth of his unpretending goodness is known only
to the God whom he worshiped in the secret of his own heart.
While in every act of his life he served him openly.
To him who gave it the Spirit has returned.
                    The dust lies here.
His children have placed this Stone To record his virtues
to his children's children.
He was born in Rockbridge Virga. Augst. 20th 1769.
And died at Chatham, near this place Feby. 2nd 1838.

Touching this spot lie the Remains of
St. George Tucker Coalter, Esqr., only son of
John Coalter, who followed his Father to the grave before
this tomb was completed. He died August 19, 1839, aged
            30 years and 2 Months and 7 days.
    A son worthy of such a father."

COALTER, ST. GEORGE TUCKER
        "St. George Tucker Coalter
            Born June 2, 1809
            Died August 12, 1839."
This small stone is adjacent to the tomb of Judge John Coalter.

COLSON, CHARLES
                Chas. Colson
                    Died
            the 17th May 1770
                Aged 66"

COOKE, MRS. EMILY M.
                "In Memory of
                Emily M. Cooke
            wife of Dr. James Cooke
            Born 12th November 1799
            Died 1st July 1832."

    Mrs. Cooke's stone is adjacent to that of William Pearson,
her father.

COX, MRS. ELIZABETH M.
                "In Memory of
                Elizabeth M.
            wife of George Cox
            who died March 15th 1831
                Aged 52 years
                  Also of
                   Eliza
            daughter of the above
            George and Elizabeth Cox
        who died August 8th 1805. Aged 14 months."

DANDRIDGE, COLONEL JOHN

"Here lies interred the Body
of Colonel John Dandridge
of New Kent County who
departed this life the 31st day
of August 1756, Aged 56 years."

DOWNMAN, JOSEPH HENRY

"Joseph Henry
infant son of
Wm. Yates & Mary Ann
Downman
Died March 26, 1857, aged 4 days."

DUFFELL, SAMUEL LEONARD

"In Memory of
Samuel Leonard Duffel
son of Edwd. & Elizabeth
Duffell who departed
this life 27th June 1803
Aged one year, 7 Months
& 2 days."

DUFFEL, SAMUEL

"In Memory of
Samuel, son of James &
Rebecca Duffel
who died 20th
August   1808
Aged 3 Months."

DUNCANSON, JAMES

"Here lies
The Body of James Duncanson
He was born in Scotland the
11th February 1735
Arrived in Virginia in July,1752
Died the 4th March 1791
'Weed his Grave clean ye Men of Goodness
'For he was your Brother'.
Sterne"

DUNCANSON, MRS. MARY

"Here lies
The Body of Mary the beloved
Wife of James Duncanson
She was born the 3d Feby. 1748
Died the 10th October 1790."

EDRINGTON, MRS. PRISCILLA
> "In memory of
> Priscilla Edrington wife of
> Edmund Edrington of this Town
> She was born the 10th Octr. 1777 &
> Died the 10th of June 1801 Aged
> 23 years and 8 months."

FISHER, JAMES
> "James Fisher
> died * September 1792
> Aged * Months
> & 15 days."

(*) These figures could not be deciphered with certainty. The entire face has disintergrated to the extent at the first glance it appears to be devoid of any letter whatever.

FORD, JOHN T., ESQ^R.
> "Sacred
> to the memory of
> John T. Ford Esqr.
> who departed this life
> June the 30th 1824
> in the 44th year of his age."

"He possessed a mind of the first order, a temper mild and benevolent and feelings exquisite and honourable.
A purer spirit never left this earthly tenement to inhabit the mansions of immortality."

FOX, SAMUEL
> "In memory of
> Samuel Fox
> who departed this
> Life March 13th 1804
> Aged 72 years."

This stone is fastly disintergrating.

GARTS, MARGARET
> "Margaret Garts
> Born
> Sept.29th 1766
> Died
> * * * ** (1789)"

The death date is imbeded in the ground. The Historical Sketch of 1892 gives 1789 as the date then appearing on this stone.

GOODWIN, ANN MARIA

                    "In Memory of
                      Our Mother
                  Ann Maria Goodwin
                        Born
                  February 18th 1775
                        Died
                  March 18th 1849
              Her record is on high."
The tombstone of Mrs. Goodwin is adjacent to that
of her parents William Smith (1746-1802) and Mary
his wife (1750-1822).

GOODWIN, CASPER WISTER

      "Sacred to the memory of Caspter Wister,
      son of Littleton and Ann Maria Goodwin,
      who departed this life at "Woodlawn",
      Spotsylvania County, on New Year's morning,
      1851, aged 13 years and 5 months.

      Be ye therefore ready
      For the son of man cometh at an hour
      That ye think not."

GOODWIN, ELIZABETH

                    "In Memory of
                      Elizabeth
                the infant daughter of
                 Thomas & Ann M.Goodwin
               who departed this life at
             6 o'clock on the Morning
               of the 3rd September 1813
             Aged 1 year, 5 months & 27 days.
                  Sleep sweet Babe
                  With angles sleep."

GOODWIN, JOHN HARWOOD

                    "Erected   .
                by an affectionate wife
                   to the memory of
                 her Lamented Husband
                     John Harwood
                    sixth son of
              T. & A. M. Goodwin
           Born on the 29th Decr. 1806
             and departed this life
           the 1st of January 1842
           aged 35 years and 2 days."

GOODWIN, MARY

> "In Memory of
> Mary Goodwin
> Born Sept, 17, 1809
> Died June 26, 1882."

GOODWIN, THOMAS

> "In Memory of
> Thomas
> the third son of Thomas
> and Ann M, Goodwin
> He was born
> on the 16th March 1800
> and departed this life
> on the 2d February 1823
> In his death we are taught
> that in the midst of life
> we are in death."

GOODWIN, THOMAS

> "Erected
> by an afflicted family
> in memory of
> Thomas Goodwin
> who was born on the
> *9th day of October 1771
> and died on the
> *14th day of January 1836."

(*) While these two days of the month are very indistinct,
I believe they are correctly deciphered.

HARRISON, MARY C.

> "In Memoriam
> Mary C.
> Harrison
> Born July 28, 1852
> Died Aug. 5, 1805
> Asleep in Jesus"

HART, CATHERINE ROSE

> "Catherine Rose
> Daughter of
> J.R. & A.M.S. Hart
> Aged 9 Mos.& 14 days."

There is footstone "C.R.H.", but no dates appear on
either stone.

HELMSTATTER, PHILIP J.

> "Sacred to the memory of
> Philip J. Helmstatter
> who died Aug. 17, 1831

next page

- continued
              Aged 31 years
         This stone is placed here
         by an affectionate Mother
            to an (***)y son."
(***) Three letters indistinct; we suspose this word
is "only".

HILDROOP, MRS. MARY
                   "In Memory of
              Mrs. Mary Hildroop
                   who died
              on the 18th Sept.1832
              in the 77th year of
                   her age."

HILL SARAH
                   "Sarah
              daughter of
              J.B. & H. Hill"
No date appear on this stone.   The Historical Sketch
of 1892 gives 1841 as the death date of this infant.

HILLYARD, PARKE G.
                   "Parke G. Hillyard
              Born October 7,   1835
              Died October 31,   1857."

HITZ, MARGARET
                   "Margaret Hitz
              Born * * *   1821
              Died July 1832"
(* * *) Undecipherable.

HULL, JOHN G. & FRANCES A.
         "Sacred to the memory of John G. Hull and
         Frances A. his wife. The former of whom died
         on the 10th day of April 1841, aged 35 years,
         and the latter on the 31st day of August 1841,
         aged 43 years.
         Blessed are the dead who die in the Lord
         Lovely and beloved in life
         In death they were not separated."

JACKSON, MICHAEL
                   "In Memory of
                   Michael
              son of Thos. & Mary A.
                   Jackson
              who died June 3rd 1802."
The above tombstone marking the grave of this infant
child, is the smallest stone in the cemetery.

JONES, JOHN

"John Jones
1752"
This is the oldest tombstone in the cemetery and
is perfectly preserved.

JOHNSTON, JANE W. & ANN THOMPSON
"In Loving Memory of
Jane W. Johnston
Born May 10, 1806
Died March 17, 1889
Until the Day Dawn."

And the other side of this monument is inscribed.
"Ann Thompson Johnston
Died October 24, 1841
Aged 74 years."

JOHNSTON, LARKIN
"In Memory of
Larkin Johnston
who departed this life
April 25th, 1831
Aged 34 years
As a slight tribute of affection for departed
worth & piety, thus humble monument is erected.

And I heard a voice from Heaven saying, with
me, Write, Blessed are the dead which die in
the Lord from henceforth Yea, saith the spirit,
that they may rest from their labours and their
worries do follow them."   Rev.14:13

KNOX, ELIZA SOMERVILLE
"Eliza Somerville
daughter of Thomas F. and Virginia
A. Knox
Died 7th Mrh. 1841
Aged 2 Mos. 12 das."

LEWIS, WILLIAM
"Here lies the body of
William Lewis who departed
this life January the 28th 1763
aged 40 years.
Also Ann his Daughter died in
1755 Aged 15 Months
And George his son died 1763
Aged 5 years."

LUCAS, JAMES W.

> "In Memory of
> James W. Lucas
> Born March 4th 1799
> Died August 23rd 1850:
> In the 52nd year of his age."

LUCAS, MRS. ELIZABETH G.

> "In Memory of
> Elizabeth G. Lucas
> Consort of
> Fielding Lucas, decd.
> Born May 10th 1780
> Died May 15th 1857."

LYON, MRS. ELIZABETH P.

> "Departed this life
> Sept.11th 1838
> Mrs. Elizabeth P.Lyon
> Aged 52 years."

McGUIRE, REV. E.C. & J.C.L.

> "Rev. Edward C.McGuire
> Born July 26, 1793
> Died Oct. 8, 1858
> J.C. Lewis
> Relict of
> Rev. E. C. McGuire
> Born Oct. 4, 1794
> Died March 26, 1882"

McGUIRE, JOHN FENTON

> "John Fenton McGuire
> son of E.C. and J.C.McGuire
> Born 4 August 1839
> Died - - - - 1841"

McPHERSON, ARCHIBALD

> "Here lyes the body of
> Archibald McPherson
> born in the County of Murray
> in North Britain, who died
> August the 17, 1754 Aged 49 years.

He was judicious, a lover of learning, openhearted,
generous and sincere. Devout without ostintation;
disdaining to cringe to vice in any Station.
Friend to good men, an affectionate husband.
"A heap of dust alone remains of Thee
> 'Tis all thou art, and all the
> proud shall be."
Elizabeth, his disconsolate widow, as testimony
of their mutual affection erected this monument
to his memory."

MARSHALL, JAMES EDGAR

"In Memory of
James Edgar Marshall
son of
Horace & Elizabeth Marshall
Born August 7th 1807
departed this life at the University of Virginia
the 5 November 1825. He was a dutiful & affectionate son and died much <u>much</u> lamented by all who
knew him."

MASON, ANNA TAYLOR (BRAXTON)

"Sacred
(here follows a four line verse not enough of
which could be deciphered to bring together
sensible words)
This Tablet
is placed here by Charles Mason in acknowledgement
of gratitude for the affectionate love of his kind
and devoted wife
Anna Taylor Mason
who died the 15th of May 1831 Aged 23 years leaving
a character distinguished for all the virtues which
exalt and adorn her so. She was the only surviving
child of Tayloe and Anna Braxton of Richmond, Virginia,
Both of whom died at an early age leaving in charge
of their friends this pledge of their affection and
when this dear object of ***** and fond devotion had
just attained the endearing affection of parent the
blighting hand of death made her husband a widower
and her infant an orphan."
(*****) Undecipherable

MAURY, MRS. CATHERINE

This large	)	"the Body of Catharine
corner	)	wife of James Maury
of the	)	Liverpool on the 22 of May 1794
stone	)	the 39th year of her age.
is broken	)	living it was her purpose
and missing	)	returned * * * among
------------------		her own People.

While dying she desire that these remains
should rest here.
She was of the best of Women."

MOODY, BRADSTREET

(5 cornered star)
"Here lies
the body of
Bradstreet Moody

next page

— — continued
                a native of Sandbarnton
                    New Hampshire
                    Who died
                    in this town
                    on the 24th Augt.
                        1827
            — — — — — — — — — — (BROKEN OFF HERE)
The bottom portion of the tombstone of Bradstreet
Moody is broken just below his death date. The
Historical Sketch of 1892 gives his age as 25 years
in their list of names and ages as taken from the
stones at that time.

NEWBY, JANE SARAH & ELIZA
    This small stone to these two infants who died in 1795
    is so badly defaced but few letters and figures can be
    deciphered with certainty.

PATTERSON, JOHN
                    "Here lies the body of
                        John Patterson
                    who died September 10th
                            1814
                    Aged 34 years."

PATTON, ANTHONY BUCK & VA.B. (COAKLEY)
                    "Sacred to the Memory of
                    Anthony Buck Patton
                    Beloved husband of
                        Virginia B. Patton
                    Died Jan.22, 1903.

                    Virginia B. Patton
                        Daughter of
                    John and Elizabeth Coakley
                        Died January 7, 1924."

PAUL, WILLIAM
                    "William Paul
                        1774"
    The stone is enclosed in a granite stone on the back
    of which is inscribed:
                    "Restored
                    23 September 1930
                    By Admirers of
                    John Paul Jones
                    Commodore U.S.N.
                        By whom
                This stone was first set in
                place in memory of William
                    his older brother."

PEARSON, JOHN B.

> "Sacred to Memory of
> John B. Pearson of Saint
> Margar -* * * * * * *who
> departed * * fe March
> * * * 04 - * *   years
> and * * * ays."

This stone is adjacent to that of Chas.M. Rothrock and
not near that of Wm. Pearson.
The entire face of it is about to fall away as has a
considerable part of the central portion of the inscription.
We presume the tombstone was in much better state of pre-
servation 50 years ago, as the Historical Sketch of 1892
gives his death date as 1804, and his age as 5 years.

PEARSON, WILLIAM

> "In Memory of
> William Pearson
> who departed this life
> on the 28th of March 1824
> in the 64th year of her age.
> Here lies interred
> William Garrett
> the son of
> William & Eleanor Pearson
> who departed this life in the
> 3d year of his age."

PILCHER, FREDERICK

> "Sacred
> To the Memory of
> Frederick Pilcher
> Born 7th of August 1769
> Departed this life
> the 13th day of April 1832
> He lived and died an honest man."

PILCHER, HIRAM

> "In Memory of
> Hiram Pilcher
> who departed this life A.D. 1833
> Aged 33 years."

PILCHER, MRS. MARGARET

> "In Memory of
> Mrs. Margaret Pilcher
> Wife of Fred: Pilcher who
> departed this life December 20, 1827
> Aged 57 years.

Her pious and dutiful life was extended to an honorable
old age and closed by an examplary death. Her charity

next page

continued
had its * * * in religion. Her love of her neighbour
was the genuine seat of her love of God. Her * * *
was the fruit of her faith and she died in hope because
she had lived a Christian."
(***) These could not be deciphered by me.

RICHARDSON, GEORGE
"Sacred
to the memory of
George Richardson
Stone Cutter
who was killed by an accident
May 12th 1807:
Aged 45 years
Stay, passenger, thy step: reflect awhile:
Tho now in health and vigour thou may smile
Tomorrows fun thy obeequies may see
The silent grave may then thy mansion be.
Then seek in life God's favour to possess
And to thy soul secure eternal happiness.

———————

Nancy daughter of the said George Richardson
and of Lucy his wife died May 29th 1802:
aged 14 months.
Jesus said, 'suffer little children, and
forbid them not, to come unto me, for of
such is the Kingdom of heaven'."

RIDDLEY, JAMES
"In Memory of
James Riddley
who departed this
Life June 19th 1800
Aged 72 years."

The entire face of this old sandstone tombstone fell off
in 1938 and no letter is now (1940) visable on the portion which is standing. This was copied a short time
before the stone disintegrated.

RITCHARDSON, MRS. WINEFRID
"Here lies the body of
Winefrid the wife of Daniel
Ritchardson who died Octr. the 16th;1763,
aged 23 years. Also 3 children lies Enterrd
by her
Remember man as you pass by
So you are now so once was I
So as I am so must you be
Therefore prepare to follow me."
This stone is next to George Richardson; note the
difference in spelling of the two names.

ROBEY, MRS. ANN

"In Memory of Ann
wife of Richard Robey
who died November 28th 1811
Aged 38 years.
The sever'd ties of kindred dear
Demand the fervant sigh
But sacred hope dries every tear
And point to bliss on high."
Footstone marked: "A.R. - 1811"

The headstone is fastly disintergrating and will not
be long legible.

ROSE, ALEXANDER

"In Memory of
Alexander Rose
of the Parish of Vere
in the Island of Jamaica
Merchant
and a native of North - Britain
who visited the United State of America
for the recovery of his health
and departed this life
at Fredericksburg in Virginia
on the 28th day of November 1800.
This stone is placed over his remains
in testimony of affectionate and
fraternal regard by his brother
William Rose of the said Island."

R., G.   and R., N.

" G. R.
1807
N. R.
1802."

These initials and dates appear on a large tombstone
adjacent to that of Chas.M.Rothrock. The Historical
Sketch of 1892 suggests that the headstone was broken
during the War Between the States when Fredericksburg
was bombed.

ROTHROCK, CHARLES M.

- - - - - - - - (Broken)
"Also Charles M. Rothrock
Departed this life Septr.
29 1084, Aged 3 years."

This gravestone is remarkable for its date, and well
preserved. For photograph see: Quinn: History of
Fredericksburg, Va., page 264.
The stone is broken, perhaps about in half, but I find
no evidence of the other portion.

next page

- - - continued
    The Historical Sketch of 1892 oddly makes no particular
    mention of this tombstone, but simply gives the death
    date of Charles W. Rothrock as 1804. However, it is
    unmistakeable - 1084.

ROTHROCK, GEORGE W.
                "George W. Rothrock
                Died December 9, 1865
                    Aged 67 years."

ROTHROCK, JEANNIE J.
                "Jeannie J. Rothrock
                Born January 22, 1830
                Died October 31, 1851
            Come Lord Jesus, Come Quickley."

ROTHROCK, LOUISIANA (JOHNSTON) & FAYETTA
                "In Loving Memory of
                Louisiana Johnston
                wife of the late
                George W. Rothrock
                Died January 25, 1888
                    Aged 84 years.

                    Fayetta
                    daughter   of
                Louisiana & George Rothrock
                        Born 1842
                        Died 1863"

SIMONS, MRS. CATHERINE
                "Here lies the Body of
                    Catherine
                the beloved wife of
                    David Simons
                who departed this life
                May 14th 1794 Aged 35 years.
                Also her two children lies
                    entered with her."

SMITH, MRS. MARY
                "In Memory of
                    Mary
                Relict of William Smith
                Born March 20, 1750
                Departed this life
                    July 8th 1822."

SMITH, WILLIAM

"Here lies the body of
William Smith
a native of Glocestershire in England
Born 25th May 1746
And departed this life October 7,1802.
An honest man is the noblest work of God."
(Note: Stones 93 & 94 & 95 are adjacent, and the oldest
interments in the Goodwin line. Mrs. Ann, wife
of Thomas Goodwin, Sr., was the daughter of
Wm. & Mary Smith.)

SMITH, WILLIAM (Jr)

"In Memory of
William
son of Wm. and Mary Smith
Born April 18, 1787
At the commencement of the late War
he entered the Army as a Lieutenant and
departed this life whilst in the service
of his country on the 30th January 1815."

SPILMAN, WALTER

"In Memory of
Walter
son of
Tho.W. & Ann Spilman
who died Feby. 12th 1837
in the 4th year of his age."

STROTHER, FRENCH

"In Memory of
French Strother
who departed this life
June 3rd 1800
Aged 61 years"

T., F * *

- - - - - - - (Broken)
Born 26 April 1812
Died the 1st Nov. 1832.
This tombstone was in this condition in 1892, but Rev.
Clark reports in his Historical Sketch of St. George
Churchyard of that date, that there was a footstone
bearing the initials "F.G.H.T." In 1940 I failed to
locate the footstone. I believe he was mistaken about
the initials on footstone so far as concerns the "GH",
and that this broken headstone belongs to Felix W.
Taliaferro whose obituary appeared as follows in the
Fredericksburg VIRGINIA HERALD of 3 November 1832:

next page

~ ~ ~ continued
"Died- on Thursday evening, 1st of November, Mr. Felix
W. Taliaferro, son of the late Mr. Hay Taliaferro, of
Orange county, aged about 20 years."

TALIAFERRO, MRS. CATHERINE (REAT)

"Catherine Taliaferro
Born
29 January 1791
Died
21st November 1869.
Blessed are the dead which died in the Lord."

THOM, CATHERINE

"Catherine Thom
died
Jan. 27, 1886."
The Historical Sketch of 1892 gives her age as 70 years
when she died.

THOM, MARY

"Mary Thom
Died June 17, 1894
Numbered with Thy Saints in Glory everlasting."

THOM, REUBEN TRIPLETT

Reuben Triplett Thom
Died May 7th 1868
Aged 85 years and 6 months.

Eleanor Reat
wife of
R. T. Thom
Died Nov.20th 1865
Aged 79 years & 4 months."
These two inscriptions on one monument.
Nearby lies their two daughters (#100, and #101) and
also Mrs. Catherine Taliaferro, whose maiden name is
given as Reat by the Historical Sketch of 1892.

WALKER, ROBERT

"Sacred
in memory of
Robert Walker
late Merchant in Fredericksburg
whose remains are here deposited
He was born near
Belfast in Ireland
the 20th day of October A.D. 1766
and departed this life
the 27th day of January 1808."

WARE, JAMES

                        "Sacred
                   to the memory of
                    James R. Ware
                  Born April 19, 1812
                   departed this life
                  September 7th 1850.
                Beloved in life and lamented
                      in death."

WARE, THOMAS

                    "In Memory of
                     Thomas Ware
                 who departed this life
                   6th August 1820
               Near this spot lies the remains
                 of William son of Thomas &
                    Catherine Ware."

WARE, THOMAS R.

                      "Thos. R. Ware
                         C.S.N."
            The Historical Sketch of 1892 registers the interment
            of Thos.R. Ware U.S.N. & C.S.N. in 1889 aged 75 years.

WHITE, HENRY GARRETT

                  "Deposited here are the remains of
                        Henry Garrett
                   son of William H. and Amanda White who
                 died 19 September 1822 aged 19 months & 11 days."

WHITFIELD   JOHN

                    "In Memory of
                  John Whitfield of
                  Whitehaven who departed
                 this life the 22nd of March
                 1766 in the 25th year of his age."

YOUNG, MRS. ELIZABETH

                    "In Memory of
                  Elizabeth Young
                     wife of
                    James Young
                 Born 22nd November 1778
                   Died 10th July 1806.
               Weep not dear friends tho I am no more
               When God thus calls its not amiss
               He bade me come
               I go before
               To meet you in eternal bliss."

INDEX

Bates			Betty	
Nancy	47		Elizabeth	26
Batley			Bibb	
Ann W.	52		Agnes P.	6
			Harriet A.	23
Baxter			Julia Ellis	46
Anne	6			
Eleanor	52		Blaxton	
			Ann	12
Beach				
Ann	58		Blythe	
			Mary	34
Beale				
Eliza S.	20		Boores	
Mary F.	20		Ellen	57
Beck			Bosel	
Jane E.	39		Emily P.	10
Mary A.	41			
			Botts	
Beckwith			Nancy	38
Elizabeth B.	11			
			Bowen	
Beech			Ann	56
Sarah	43			
			Bowling	
Belfour			Nancy	47
Jane	53			
			Boyle	
Bell			Mary Ann	61
Susan	58			
			Bradshaw	
Bennett			Frances Ann	30
Lucy	35			
			Bragdon	
Benson			Elizabeth	21
Catharine E.	60			
Elizabeth	54		Bridwell	
Harriet	24		Mary	26
Judith A.	3			
Judith	47		Briggs	
			Charlotte U.	59
Berry			Mary H.	49
Catherine H.	4			
Maria M.	37		Briscoe	
Rosa Ann	34		Jane	10
			Susan Ann	47
Bertier				
Frances J.	33			

Brock	
Julia Anne	59
Brooke	
Fenton	48
Grace Fenton	48
Lucy	52
Brooks	
Clarissa T.	44
Brown – Browne	
Cytha	30
Elizabeth	31
Emily M.	6
Louisa	4
Maria	36
Mary	21,42
Mary Ann	9
Milly Stone	35
Nancy	44
Brownlow	
Susan Frances	44
Brumfield	
Elizabeth	59
Mary	45
Bryant	
Catharine	54
Elizabeth	44
Margaret P.	11
Buck	
Harriet S.	40
Margaret	48
Mary Miller	48
Bullard	
Ann F.	17
Bunberry	
Elizabeth S.	39
Bundy	
Eliza	18
Burden	
Eliza	36
Lucy Ann	60
Susan	37

Burke	
Mary Ann	19
Mary B.	20
Burnett	
Elizabeth	16
Emily	29
Mary	38
Burnley	
Mary	7
Burton	
Catherine Elizabeth	24
Philippa	18
Butler	
Maria	30
Byram	
Betty M.	29
Elizabeth	10
Eliza	28
Mary	38

C

Caldwell	
Ariana	11
Elizabeth	25
Margaret	55
Calhoun	
Grace	14
Mary	12
Sophia	6
Callet	
Elizabeth	61
Calvert	
Nancy	5
Carmichael	
Ann	23
Ann F. L.	28
Jannett Gordon	19
Carpenter	
Sarah E.	10

Coyle		Curry	
Elizabeth	9	Judith	7
Crawford		**D**	
Caroline	1		
Jane B.	4	Dabney	
Martha	50	Sarah Ann	29
Mary Wilson	25	Susan H.	31
Cridlen – Cridlin		Dade	
Jane Alice	52	Eliza B.	45
Mary E.	22	Nancy	3
Crissey		Daingerfield	
Ann Maria	35	Mildred	41
		Sarah Jane	44
Crosley – Crossley			
Jane Gaskins	21	Daniel	
Mary	50	Elizabeth	29
		Frances E. L.	28
Crump		Sarah	42
Ann M.	24		
Ann Eliza	25	Dare	
May	59	Ann M.	27
Crutchfield		Davis	
Mildred E.	35	Agnes	19
		Elizabeth	40
Cudlipp		Frances	42, 45
Eliza	37	Letitia	5
		Sally	47
Cunningham			
Ann	28	Day	
Mary	10	Christiana Yates	4
		Elizabeth	43
Cuppenhaven		Sally	11
Mary	57	Susannah	7
Curtis		De Baptiste	
Ann	37	Lucinda	17
Catharine	26	Polly	3
Mary Ann	34	Virginia	51
Susanna Jane	54		
		Dickey	
Curran		Ann Eliza	12
Catharine	42	Frances	5
Currell		Dillard	
Mary Ann	1	Eliza A.	59
Mary	19		

Ferrell
　Melinda　　　　　61

Ficklin
　Ann Eliza　　　　25
　Ellen Douglas　　6

Finnall
　Angelina S.　　　20
　Jane　　　　10, 11
　Mary Ann McD　　11

Fisher
　Eliza M.　　　　8
　Maria　　　　　34

Fitchett
　Betsy　　　　　19
　Delia　　　　　21

Fitzgerald
　Elizabeth T.　　54

Fitzhugh
　Ann F.　　　　33
　Caroline M.　　53
　Harriet W.　　13
　Mary P. B.　　50

Flack
　Sarah　　　　　41

Ford
　Frances　　　　51
　Jane　　　　　54
　Sophia　　　　51

Fortune
　Margaret　　　58

Fountain
　Mary　　　　　14

Frazer
　Ann　　　　　32
　Eleanor　　　48
　Lucy Ann　　　49
　Philadelphia C.　55

French
　Anne　　　　　45
　Mary　　　　　37

Fries
　Catharine　　40

Frye
　Elizabeth　　28

Fugett
　Orphy L.　　54

G

Gaines
　Matilda　　　24
　Sophia　　　11

Garder - Gardner
　Caroline　　53

Garetson
　Mary　　　　54

Garner
　Clementine　52
　Eliza　　　60
　Fenton　　　26
　Louise　　　9

Garnett
　Eliza F.　　57
　Louisa C. T.　3
　Malvina　　　1
　Margaret　　55

Garton
　Mary　　(2)　12

Gaskins
　Mary E.　　28

Gibbs
　Mary Virginia　20
　Sally　　　　6

Godfrey
　Mary M.　　57
　Sarah G.　　45

Goodwin
    Ann M. S.   23
    Elizabeth   19
    Evelina C. S.   23

Gordon
    Agnes Campbell   2
    Marion   52
    Mary N.   56
    Susan F.   20, 45
    Susan H.   53

Gore
    Frances   2
    Elizabeth H.   2

Grady
    Leanah   38
    Nancy   26
    Rebecca   28

Graham
    Catharine   43
    Sarah R.   25
    Susanna Sidney   50

Grant
    Lydia   31

Graves
    Lucy Ellen   36

Gray
    Ann   13
    Emma N.   8

Green
    Eliza   21
    Elizabeth   27
    Harriet   23
    Jane   37
    Judith   6
    Mary   12
    Rebecca S.   35
    Virginia V.   24

Gregory
    Fanny Scott   10
    Patsey   17

Grigsby
    Eliza   21

Grinnan
    Ann Grigsby   60

Grotz
    Betty   41
    Margaret C.   44
    Nancy   41

Griffin
    Elizabeth   39

Guthridge
    Mary Ann   40

Guthrie
    Rosey   26

· H

Hall
    Charlotte   22
    Julia A.   23
    Maria   60
    Mary Harrison   19
    Sarah   21
    Sophia   21

Hackley
    Lucia B.   37

Hagan
    Catharine   38

Haner
    Mary   1

Hanson
    Sarah A.   3

Harpe
    Patsey   5

Harris
    Sarah   5

Harrod
    Dorothy   33

Harvey
  Sarah   12

Haydon
  Ann V.   57

Haywood
  Sarah Franklin   15

Hazelgrove
  Elizabeth   11

Head
  Mary   33

Heiskell
  Anna Maria   27
  Caroline   19
  Elizabeth   35

Helmstetter - Helmistatter
  Mary Ann   12
  Susan P.   23

Henderson
  Jane   57
  Mary   38

Henry
  Catherine   47
  Rebecca M.   18

Herard
  Claude Victorine   30

Herndon
  Amanda M.   50
  Jane Whittier   50

Heslep
  Sarah   42

Hewlitt
  Mary   47
  Nancy   3

Hildrup
  Elizabeth   20

Hill
  Charlotte   46

Hill (continued)
  Jane   55
  Mary   4

Hillyard
  Sarah Ann   25

Hogan
  Ellen Frances   22

Holbrook
  Clarissa   17
  Phebe   29

Hollinger
  Husley   31

Holt
  Virginia F.   60

Hooten
  Eliza   30

Hord
  Harriot   3
  Mary   9

Hore
  Mary   9

Howard
  Matilda   19

Howison
  Ann M.   53
  Helen M.   53
  Jane B.   3
  Marian   50

Huggins
  Mary   33

Hughlett
  Catherine   15
  Judah   43
  Mildred   52
  Nancy   48

Kent
    Frances A.   8

Kersey
    Caroline H.   42

Keys – Keyes
    Christiana   42
    Lucy   37

King
    Catharine A.   36
    Eloise M.   29
    Martha Ann   49
    Maria B.   11
    Mary   21, 27
    Mary M.   46
    Sarah   13, 61

Knight
    Ann   22
    Polly   18

Knox
    Agnes G.   49

L

Lane
    Maria M.   11

Lawson
    Elizabeth   1
    Ellen   54
    Lucinda   54

Layton
    Elizabeth   2
    Isabella   53
    Lucy   13
    Lydia Ann   44
    Martha A.   38
    Mildred   60
    Ophelia   27
    Rebecca Frances   29
    Unus   18

Leach
    Sarah   30

Lear
    Alice   (2)   16

Lee
    Amanda   43
    Mary   2

Lefene
    Mary S.   46

Lewis
    Ann Eliza   25
    Betty   38
    Betty B.   3
    Eliza   13
    Elizabeth   55
    Ellen   1
    Fanny   43
    Judith C.   33
    Maria   25, 27
    Mary   16
    Mary A. E.   7
    Pamelia   21

Limbrick
    Susan   37

Lindsay
    Jean   45

Lithgow
    Mary W.   39

Little
    Mary A.   46

Lomax
    Ann Maria   30
    Cornelia   55
    Ellen T.   30
    Martha   44

Long
    Elizabeth   16
    Lucretia   26
    Malvira   44
    Maria Louisa   55
    Mary Jane   46
    Mary S.   20
    Virginia   57

Lorimer			McTyre	
Virginia	33		Sally	50
Lowery			McWhirt	
Jane L.	55		Barbara	22
Lucas			McWilliams	
Ann	32		Julia	6
Ann A.	56		Mary	47
Elizabeth	17			
Ellen	16		**M**	
Martha E.	58			
Mary W.	4		Mackay	
Rebecca C.	32		Eliza Jane	60
Sally	20			
Sarah	54		Magee	
			Sucky	34
Lyon				
Emily	26		Magrath	
			Julia M.	5
Lymbrick				
Mary	3		Mahoney	
			Peggy	6
Mc				
			Mann	
McCarty			Fanny	9
Laura E.	42		Polly	16
McFarlane			Mardes	
Elizabeth	56		Emily	49
Jane	35			
Mary Ann	34		Mark	
			Eleanor	48
McGuire				
Mary Ann	9		Martin	
			Harriet E.	25
McIntosh				
Isabella	41		Massey	
Jenetta	38		Ellen	41
McKeen			Matthews – Mathews	
Flora	19		Charlotte D.	24
			Phiana H.	56
McKildoe				
Mary S.	10		Mattison	
			Ellen	29
McKnight				
Ruth	4		Maury	
			Matilda H.	15
McPherson			Willa S.	21
Elizabeth	9			
Mary	38			

Penny
  Elizabeth   49

Perry
  Georgiana   29
  Lucinda   15,17
  Mary Frances   23
  Mary J.   51
  Pamelia   36

Peters
  Lucy   28

Peyton
  Jane J.   54
  Sarah   35

Phillips
  Ann T.   18
  Elizabeth W.   40
  Emily L.   7
  Julia A.   33
  Louisa Mildred   57
  Pamelia   51

Pilcher
  Eliza   60
  Mary A.   13

Pitman
  Mary   37

Pitts
  Maria   46

Pollard
  Judith   39

Poole
  Agnes   29

Pope
  Mary   49
  Sarah Ann   38

Porch - Portch
  Angelina   5
  Charlotte   47
  Susan   26

Porter
  Cassandra   29

Powell
  Lavinia   14
  Mary Somerville   27

Pratt
  Harriot   61

Pritchard
  Ann   53
  Margaret   48

Proctor
  Ann   25
  Susan Elizabeth   53

Pullen - Pullin
  Elizabeth   20
  Lucy Ann   36
  Sarah   57

Purcell
  Margaret A. L.   45

Purks
  Eliza   37

Pusey - Puzey
  Elizabeth   17
  Mildred   47
  Shady   36

Q

Quisenberry
  Virginia L.   47

R

Ragan
  Frances   58

Raines
  Mary Ann   46

Ralls
  Mary   24

Randall
  Matilda   28

Rasor
  Mary   18

Rawlins	
Sarah	8
Reat	
Catherine	56
Redd	
Martha P.	15
Reeves	
Elizabeth	58
Lucinda (2)	41
Rennolds	
Elizabeth	46
Reveer	
Fanny	52
Jane	23
Richards	
Elizabeth	21
Evelina	16
Julia	8
Sarah H.	49
Susan Ann	30
Richardson	
Mary Ann	1
Patsy	57
Sarah Ann	2
Ridley	
Elinor	2
Mary Ann	34
Riley	
Ann E.	53
Mary	19
Robey	
Harriet	31
Robertson	
Lelia	48
Robinson	
Elizabeth	50
Roddy	
Sidney Smith	56

Rollow	
Eliza Ann	19
Sarah W.	60
Rootes	
Ann F.	36
Mary R.	20
Sarah	9
Rose	
Jane	24
Mary	26
Sarah C.	56
Susan	44
Rothrock	
Elizabeth W.	5

S

Sacrae	
Fanny	56
Sanger	
Elizabeth	16
Saunders	
Elizabeth	38
Scags	
Elizabeth	58
Margaret R.	2
Scales	
Maria	18
Scott	
Ann	4
Janet H.	22
Susanna E. M.	21
Seddon	
Ann	45
Leah	51
Marion	49
Mary L.	46
Seldon	
Elizabeth A.	29
Semmes	
Sarah Wilhemina	38

Sexsmith
    Eliza   47
    Mary   29

Shears
    Sarah   14

Shellings
    Eleanor   42

Shelton
    Harriet O.   36

Shepherd
    Eliza   42

Short
    Martha   28

Shuletice
    Eliza Ann   44

Sibley
    Elizabeth   42

Simpson
    Ann   16

Sindall
    Sarah   37

Slater
    Ann   55
    Eliza   14
    Harriet   5

Slaughter
    Sarah A.   17

Smallwood
    Anne   58

Smith
    Alzira   21
    Eliza   23
    Elizabeth H.   9
    Frances   13
    Frances E.   15
    Margaret   58
    Maria Ann   33
    Mary Virginia   31
    Tacy A.   5

Smock
    Elizabeth   58
    Maria   19

Snow
    Ann   45

Snipe
    Mary   40

Solivan
    Elizabeth   41

Sorrell — Sorelle
    Jane P.   60
    Mary E.   56

Southard (see Suthard)
    Harriet   11
    Jane   60
    Julia Ann   7
    Mary   40

Sparks
    Maria   3

Spencer
    Hannah   34

Spilman
    Sophia R.   37

Staiars — Staiar
    Eleminey   49
    Malvina P.   12

Stanard
    Ann H.   47
    Marie Louise   51
    Polly   51
    Virginia   48

Staylor
    Susan   10

Steigar
    Mary   30

Sterling
    Elizabeth   8

Thornton
    Charlotte Belson   31
    Martha S.   17
    Maria   51

Timberlake
    Elizabeth J.   13
    Margaret G.   1

Tomlin
    Fanny Dulany   37
    Mary L.   16

Tombs - Toombs
    Betsy   16
    Mary   26

Towles
    Adeline   19
    Eliza M.   58
    Virginia E.   37

Trainer
    Maria   42

True
    Martha   54
    Mary Jane   41
    Sarah   45
    Sarah A.   51

Truslow
    Ann   30

Tucker
    Ann   40

Turner
    Maria   44

U

Underwood
    Virginia Ann   43

V

Vass
    Ann Thornton   9
    Eliza   32
    Mary   9

Verone
    Caroline H.   7

Vessells
    Maria   7

Victor
    Harriet   14
    Lucy   27

W

Waddell
    Sarah   51

Waite
    Elizabeth   38

Walker
    Elizabeth Ann   18
    Hannah   48
    Jane   35
    Mahaley   51
    Mahallen Ann   51
    Mildred B.   53
    Sarah A.   54
    Susanna   9

Waller
    Lucy F.   7

Wardell
    Harriet H.   15
    Louisiana   55

Ware
    Alice   10
    Catharine   51

Warfield
    Fanny   47

Warren
    Susan   28

Webb
    Clara   3
    Milly   30

Webster
    Catharine   14

Wright (continued)

			Y	
Jane	5			
Mary Ann H.	4	Young		
Patsey	34	Elizabeth	5
		Frances S.	34
Wroughton		Mary	25
Henrietta	35	Mary L.	6
		Susannah B.	49
Wren - Wrenn			
Mahala Ann	28		
Mildred	52		
Selina L.	28		
Wyatt			
Sarah	32		

*****************\
****

Books by Mrs. Knorr

Marriage Bonds and Ministers' Returns of Prince Edward Co. Virginia
1754 - 1810 (1950)

Marriage Bonds and Ministers' Returns of Charlotte Co. Virginia
1764 - 1815 (1951)

Marriage Bonds and Ministers' Returns of Sussex Co. Virginia
1754 - 1810 (1952)

Marriage Bonds and Ministers' Returns of Brunswick Co. Virginia
1750 - 1810 (1953)

Marriage Bonds and Ministers' Returns of Fredericksburg, Virginia
1782 - 1850 (1954)

Each $5.00 net, postpaid.

www.ingramcontent.com/pod-product-compliance
Lightning Source LLC
Chambersburg PA
CBHW072149020426
42334CB00018B/1932